158 Oda
Life Is a Garden : The 7
Spiritual Principles of
Manifesting Every Area of Your
Life.
Oda Ph D, John P.

Life is a Garden:

The 7 Spiritual Principles of manifesting every area of your life

John P. Oda, Ph.D.

Published by BookLocker.com, Inc., Bradenton, Florida.

Printed on acid-free paper.

BookLocker.com, Inc.
2016

First Edition

Dedicated to my loving father,
Odessa Joseph Oda Sr.
(January 17, 1923 - April 2, 2014).

I have fought the good fight to the end. I have run the race to the finish I have kept the faith. **Timothy 4:7**

DISCLAIMER

The author and publisher are providing this book and its contents on an "as is" basis and make no representations or warranties of any kind with respect to this book or its contents. The author and publisher disclaim all such representations and warranties, including warranties of merchantability and fitness for a particular purpose. In addition, the author and publisher do not represent or warrant that the information accessible via this book is accurate, complete or current.

The statements made about products and services have not been evaluated by the U.S. Food and Drug Administration. They are not intended to diagnose, treat, cure, or prevent any condition or disease. Please consult with your own physician or healthcare specialist regarding the suggestions and recommend-dations made in this book.

Except as specifically stated in this book, neither the author or publisher, nor any authors, contributors, or other representatives will be liable for damages arising out of or in connection with the use of this book. This is a comprehensive limitation of liability that applies to all damages of any kind, including (without limitation) compensatory; direct, indirect or consequential damages; loss of data, income or profit; loss of or damage to property and claims of third parties.

You understand that this book is not intended as a substitute for consultation with a licensed healthcare practitioner, such as your physician. Before you begin any healthcare program, or change your lifestyle in any way, you will consult your physician or other licensed healthcare practitioner to ensure that you are in good health and that the examples contained in this book will not harm you.

This book provides content related to topics about weight loss, nutrition and health. As such, use of this book implies your acceptance of this disclaimer.

HERE IS WHAT THE EXPERT IS SAYING:

"With a style all his own and vigor that inspires others to take action, John is a true crusader for assisting others in making a positive change in their lives. The lives of those they love. I'm proud to call him a friend. My wish for you is that you too will come to work with him, and know him as well. Dr. Oda will add ten times the value. I guarantee it!"

- Joseph McClendon III, co-author with Anthony Robbins on two bestselling books and a UCLA instructor

HERE IS WHAT CLIENTS ARE SAYING ABOUT DR. JOHN ODA:

"John Oda has been my business coach for the past eight months. He has taught me strategies to take my business to the next level. Johns' time management structures have helped me increase my business dramatically without increasing my hours dramatically. What sets John apart from other coaches is his ability to help me grow as a person as well as a business owner. He teaches that a healthy mind, body and personal life are extremely important

foundations for a healthy growing business. The hidden treasure in Johns coaching is his ability to shift you to a mindset of success. A coaching session with John Oda is tantamount to a coaching session with Anthony Robbins, Napoleon Hill and Joseph McClendon III all rolled into one. The guy knows his stuff.

Oh by the way, I employ 10 great people and, in the last eight months my business has doubled, my NET PROFIT is up 120% and we're just getting warmed up. Thanks mate."

-Rob Heidemanns, Canberra, Australia

"We wanted to say, "Thank you!" During the time you have been coaching us, NeuroQuest has achieved so much more than what we had been doing on our own. As small business owners and having worked for a fortune 500 companies for many years, we were hesitant to work with a coach. Not only did we think we had all the answers, but as with any upstart, we were short on cash. We're so glad you were persistent and patient with us. Your coaching has enabled us to gain clarity in our business and personal life which has translated into massive progress and success.

We know this is only the beginning! We have found that through your direction, focus and the challenge to think outside the box we have secured more contracts, increased our orders and collections, as well as help us overcome a partnership issue we had been floundering in. The confidence we have in you and your coaching style along with the excitement you help generate will take us to the next level of success and company security. Anyone serious with either their company success or personal success needs you as their coach. Thanks Coach, the results in our business have already paid for the coaching!" In the last two years my business has increase over 900%.

-Christy Norton, President and Leslie Chase

"Dear John Oda

I just want to give you some feedback after our UGP Coaching sessions. They were excellent and I would recommend you, and have recommended you, to business owners. I used a lot of your tips and one main one which grew one part of my business 15% over 8 weeks... and it is still growing - that was the re-activation letter in combination with a special invitation to join our Inner Sanctum. The Inner Sanctum is like a Platinum group of clients who enjoy special offers, new launch invites etc. Pretty much as for other types of business but not so common in Cosmetic Medicine. Your coaching really revitalised my enthusiasm for my business which extended to an increase in my team's enthusiasm. Again, many thanks John."

-Deirdre Tozer MD, Cosmetic Surgery Specialist, Australia

"I am the owner of a busy Chiropractic/ Massage/Physical Therapy office and have been working with John Oda from Business Breakthroughs International for only about one month. Since that time we have had a 50% increase in revenues and John has structured systems to bring all of our accounts receivables current totaling over $100,000. I had reservations about joining Business Breakthroughs International, but now after

completing only the first month, I don't know how any business could afford not to join."

-Dr. Duddey, Sports Care Center

HERE IS WHAT PARENTS AND TEENS ARE SAYING ABOUT DR. JOHN ODA:

I came in hurt and came out cured. I am happier after the program than I felt in my entire life. My entire life has changed, and my school work improved."

-Fantasia, middle school student from Portland Maine

I met Dr John Oda through our pastor. He handed me a copy of Connecting with your Teen. I ate it up. It was the beginning of a transformation for my son and our family. My son was very intelligent and was given the opportunity to excel in a college prep high school-private high school and public high school-He rejected them all-and was asked to leave. He chose drugs instead. It has been a nightmare, yet Dr John Oda has coached us through all the different chapters. His knowledge of the teen mind set is very accurate. His insights should be taught worldwide. Parents, Grandparents, Aunts, Uncles, friends need help in dealing with this unspoken and ignored arena of the development of a human being. Dr Oda knows and teaches a teenager how to make a 180 degree turn around.

PSS... Dear Dr John Oda, THANK YOU for what you have given us our son, our family back, our lives back.

Yours truly,

Grace N
Michigan City, Indiana

"In spite of our burned out skepticism, we notice subtle changes in his attitude immediately. By the second week, it was if his metabolism had sped up. He was actually doing his homework unprompted and pitching in on his homework chores. We are witnessing what appears to be nothing more than a transformation. Dr. Oda you are a true miracle worker."

-Tom, Parent, Portland Oregon

"This program really helps. Words can't describe how it helps. You take the pressure off my shoulders. It's like having two football players on your back, and then you're removing them. You're like another dad sometimes. Thanks for the seven techniques."

-Griffin, a high school student from Portland Oregon

Peak performance expert, Dr. John Oda has been a great influence in changing my life and organizational skills. His time management system that he introduced to me was easy to insert my daily schedule because of the easy step by step method. Declaring my desire/goal was my first step into the organized action plan. Before I used the Oda time management system my GPA was in the low 2.0's after one term of executing my written goals under the system, my actions lead a 3.4 GPA. To this day I still use the Oda Method and would recommend anyone who wants to accomplish goals in a timely manner to use this tool.

Sincerely,

Robert (Case #5 Connecting With Your Teen) University of Oregon, Pilot

"My daughter feels that her participation in this program has allowed her to learn more about herself and how to achieve her goals more effectively. I have to admit that her beliefs are more definitely on target. Your class has helped my daughter pursue her goals in a more effective way. I feel that she always knew what she wanted, but teenagers tend to listen to other people better than parents. I am glad that the person was YOU, because you are a highly motivated individual with a lot of teenager outlook in your persona. Please provide me with information about your session to come, because we would like to participate again."

-Marcela, Parent, Beaverton Oregon

"Thank you! Thank you for being born! Thank you for loving your job! Thank you for loving yourself. And thank you for helping me."

-Heather, a high school student from Oregon

Table of Contents

Foreword by Carl Scott MPH

It is a great honor to be included in this body of work from Dr. John Oda. I have had the pleasure of working with Dr. Oda for over 25 years. My first encounter with Dr. Oda was in the mental health field working with adolescents at a psychiatric inpatient hospital.

When I met John Oda the nursing staff told me that John doesn't have any background experience working in the mental health field, and that he has a chip on his shoulder and a bad attitude, which makes him not a good fit for the field. At this time I was trying to create my own residential unit and needed staff members. When I first met John Oda, I saw a lot of raw talent and a person who wanted to achieve success in the mental health field.

I took him on as one of my staff members, and we had bi-monthly supervision to deal with his concepts, and how to professionally deal with all the patients. It took a very short period of time to find out that he had a special gift. I assisted him in honing his skills and I had to craft his skills to make John see his true potential. I would ask John to work crazy shifts days, evenings and mid nights, and without a beat he would say no problem, and he always volunteered to provide the patients with group therapy for hours because he has an insatiable appetite for learning.

John would horn on his skills by attending Anthony Robbins seminars and providing the skill set far beyond any employee I had on my staff. John's passion for always learning and demanding to be the best, and his passion for going the extra mile became contagious for everyone around him.

As I look back I now see all the seeds John planted 25 or more years ago, because it made him into the person he is today. It's an honor for any son to write a book about what their father taught him, I am a father of 8 children and I would feel honored to have my child share to the world what I taught them.

John weaves a web of how to plant the right seed, and a positive harvest will grow, and the seven pillars to creating growth in every area of your life.

1. Have Faith
2. Having the proper mindset
3. Strategy
4. Time Management
5. Passion
6. Having an attitude of gratitude
7. The Desire to serve others in the highest way

These powerful concepts are the true foundation of Life is a Garden. Dr. John Oda also creates a spiritual side mixed in with personal development to create a powerful book.

Dr. John Oda loves to learn, so he will have you learn after every chapter he will give a review of each chapter and questions because his outcome is to have you create success now in your life.

What made me a believer in Dr. John Oda, his passion to listen and then take massive action? I was fascinated by his insatiable appetite for learning and his non-stop quest to increase his skills in order to improve the lives of others. As he grew into this giant in the field of healthcare and business growth development, he obtained his PH.D. Through his research and love for this work, John has become renowned in the areas of business coaching and the significant growth of fortune 500 companies.

He calls me his mentor, I call him my inspiration!

As you turn the pages of this book, you will agree, it will inspire you!!

Carl Scott, Former CEO, Business Coach Professional

This book is a metaphor of what my father taught me about the garden he loved so much. Life is a Garden focuses on the seeds that I planted as a child and how they grew. We will explore many other spiritual principles so you can manifest every area of your life.

It is my hope that in writing this book I will give you the tools to change every area of your life. It's an honor to share with you what my father taught me and I am excited to teach you how you can use the same tools to change every area of your life. You can apply this book in your business, relationship, health, and career and even for finding your soul mate.

I learned so much about life and who I am from a garden. The garden is a metaphor and because I worked in this garden like my life depended on it, I realized that when I applied these same principles to my life; my life would never be the same

Now, here is my story.

Dr. John Oda's Story

I grew up in Michigan City, Indiana, about 45 minutes west of Chicago. My parents are originally from Mississippi. As a child my mother always wanted to live close to a beach and have ten children. By the grace of God, my parents moved to Michigan City in the year1946 and had ten beautiful children.

My father had a huge garden. My brothers and I worked outside with our father while my sisters didn't work in the garden at all. At times they went in the garden to just sit down and talk to my father. They would mainly take care of household chores.

My father planted everything a person can imagine in his garden. The garden had so many mosquitoes and they would bite our arms and legs. There were also huge spiders and worms. At night, we had lightning bugs and ants. In short, we had every possible insect in my father's garden!

The most amazing thing about my father is that he had two full time jobs. He worked 16 hours per day for five days. On the weekends he would devote all of his time to his second job: his garden. I would see him wake up at 4:30am in the morning to work on his garden. He wanted his garden to be the best and he was aware that a lot of effort needed to be put in order to make that happen.

Right from my childhood days and even as an adult, I never saw my father complain about work at all. He loved his work to the core. As a dutiful son, I would wake up every morning in the summer time from about 4:30 to 6:00am to make sure the garden was watered.

My father would plant his garden around Easter time every year, or may I say on Good Friday. In the Midwest, the weather is not the greatest during Easter time. It is the end of winter and beginning of the spring season. Before my father would plant his garden, my brother and I would make sure that the garden area was thoroughly cleaned. We had to dig out the garden with shovels and also get the collard green stems. This was not only a tough task, but also something that had to be done with utmost care. Once we were done with cleaning the garden, our father would tell us to dig out the garden so he could plant the seeds. Digging involved using the tiller. Since we were young and inexperienced at using the tiller, our father would guide us.

Since our garden was quite huge, I would ask for help from my next door neighbor, Jerry Mitchell, and other's around the neighborhood. We would do our best to dig out this garden. After we would dig it out, my father and his friend would use a tiller several times so that he could plant by Good Friday.

My father gardened every year until he had a successful garden. He fed the family delicious organic vegetables and fruit. I sometimes wondered if we could take the same metaphor of "Life is a garden." When I look back at the seeds I planted, they grew in negative and positive ways. Let me share with you now a story about how a nun planted seeds in my own life and how I manifested in a negative way.

My six sisters, three brothers and I went to St. Mary's Grade School. I had a severe stuttering problem. I could, however, speak without any problem to my friends and family (maybe because I felt very relaxed among them). At times I couldn't even say my name and I felt so embarrassed because other children around me spoke without any issues.

When I was in the first grade, I had this very mean class teacher who was a nun. She had many rules about what you could do, and even more rules about what you couldn't do. I was so scared of her; she never smiled and she was very serious all the time. Many times she would ask me to read out loud and when I read, other children would laugh at me, call me retarded and make fun of me.

One day the nun told me she wanted to meet my mother. After a couple of days my mother came to the school. My mother worked a full-time night shift at St. Anthony's Hospital. So, one day after school my mother met the nun and she was familiar with her because she had taught some of my other siblings in previous years. My mother asked the nun if she wanted me to wait outside the room. The nun stated "No," so I stayed in the room. I had previously never been part of serious discussions with grown people, as at my house that was something that never took place. The nun told my mother that the other kids in my class get along with people well. Then she went on to tell my mother I was retarded and suggested that she admit me to a school down the road called Garfield. She even felt that I would never even finish eighth grade if I continued studying in my current school. I was completely in shock. I never expected her to say something like this. She planted a huge seed in my mind. It's natural to believe words coming out from a person of authority.

My mother told the nun, "If John has to leave St Mary's, his brothers and sisters who studied in the same school would follow suit." Hearing this, the nun thought about the monetary loss that the school would incur and decided to keep me in the school on one condition; I would have to take speech therapy. Shortly after that meeting, I met my speech therapist whose name was Mr. Anderson. He was a nice gentleman who would greet people by saying: "Hi my name is Mr. Anderson, I stutter."

I told myself that I would never say anything like that because I was embarrassed that I stuttered in the first place; why would I ever mention it to the world? Mr. Anderson told me to say "real--- ize" by breaking it apart in two separate phrase/words. I thought to myself that I *would* be retarded speaking like he was telling me to. I went to speech therapy class twice a week for about 4-5 years and we would do a whole lot of things like jumping jacks, sit ups and a lot of exercise. I guess all these activities were to build up my self-esteem.

I always had this question at the back of my mind as to why only I had to do speech therapy and not my classmates. Mr. Anderson did his best at helping me with my stuttering problem, although at times I was confused and did not know to speak the way he taught me or would just attempt to push through my stuttering. For example, if I was attempting to say the word "car" I would sound like "ccccccar" because the words just did not come out! Mr. Anderson would ask me to say "My name is John, I stutter."

I found this weird as I had never seen people introducing themselves, "Hello my name is ____, I have cancer." I really believe the words you use shape your destiny and you need to choose your words carefully. I did not want to create my identity inside of being a person who stutters.

Despite abiding by all the rules, the following year I returned back to first grade again! I felt awful. I really felt that there was seriously some problem within me because even after getting 90% positive marks, I somehow still had to repeat the same grade again!

The children would mock and call me "O-DA, you are so stupid why aren't you in the second grade with us?" At that point I couldn't give them a reason at all. I really didn't know and everyone I spoke with couldn't tell my parents of why I was in first grade again.

My first grade teacher this time around was Mrs. Resteck. To make matters worse, we had first and second grade in the same classroom, so I was constantly getting teased a lot by my previous class mates. At that time I had so much anger and depression. I kept wondering and would question God; why me? What did I do to deserve this?

My mother was an angel sent by God. She was an inspiration for me. She would tell me that my father stuttered, my grandfather stuttered and they all overcame it, and so would I. Those seeds my mother planted stayed with me for the rest of my life. When I would have a bad day, I would remember the seeds my mother planted with me at such a young age.

My third grade teacher, Mrs. Kutch was a young blonde and a very nice woman by nature. I remember one day she wanted me to read a book. I told Mrs. Kutch that I could not read. She told me to take my time and read. She waited for about ten minutes. It seemed like hours for me. She told the other children not to laugh at me. This was the first teacher who took her time with me and really wanted me to succeed in life. I remember staying after class and speaking with her about my dreams in life. Every time, she encouraged me to be the best I could be. I really appreciated her love and support.

My fourth grade teacher was Mrs. Jones. At a young age my father taught me my multiplication tables. I was an expert in saying times tables and would beat everyone to the answer. This is what I excelled in so much. I remember one day, I came in from the playground early and Mrs. Jones was speaking to one of the teachers. I overheard her saying "I feel sorry for John Oda, can you imagine growing up stuttering, and he can't even read well, how he will make in this world?"

Those words hurt, like someone punched me in my stomach over and over again.

Mr. Jones lived down the street and he had two sons. When I was in my fifth grade, my father always told me not to hang out with the Jones brothers as they were trouble makers. I remember one time we were riding our bikes and I had a three speed bike while they had a ten speed one. It seemed that they were messing with this white man about 35 years old, teasing him and calling him names. At that point, I didn't know what exactly was going on. The only thing I remember is that all of a sudden the man starts chasing me on my bike and I had this blank expression on my face trying to understand what caused him to chase me! The Jones brothers were laughing as I was trying to pedal to save my dear life. The white man caught me on my bike, called me some racial slurs and punched me in my stomach. I went home and told my mother about what happened. She immediately called the police. The police arrived and I told them everything that took place. They told me that they will register a report and investigate further. After a few days, we called the police station to find out if they were able to trace that white man.

The police did trace him but stated that the man denied of doing anything to me. The police believed the man and set him free.

My sixth grade teacher was a blessing from God, very positive, nice and encouraging; exactly what the doctor had ordered. At this time I grew to be around six foot. I started playing basketball with my coach, Coach May, who was a great role model.

My sixth grade teacher would always encourage me to read out each and every word loud even if it took time. She told me that I would grow up to be a great person. She planted so many positive seeds in my garden that when I reflex back now, I see why I grew so much in confidence and self-esteem. She adored me so much that she even named her baby after me! It was such an honor for me. Her son should be 38 or 39 years old now.

During my eighth grade year, I went to California to see my two older brothers. My brother Joe stayed in the OC (35 years ago OC was called Santa Ana). I really felt very confident at this time in my life. I won a dance contest at Disneyland, and my life appeared to be taking off. I remember during my eighth grader year I must have been around 6'5 and my basketball skills were improving a lot. One day coming home I went to play some basketball with some children. I played many a times with my brother and cousins. This time I was all alone and so I beat them pretty good. It was getting late, so I told them that I had to go home. On my way home, I noticed that the kids I played with were behind me and they were going in the same direction as me.

I thought that their home must have been in the same direction. Then I got nervous so I took a shortcut to in order to get home more quickly. To my surprise, two of them were behind me and three were coming in front of me. They asked me to give them my money. At first, I thought these guys were joking because I played basketball with them many times.

I refused.

One of them pointed a gun to my head and pulled the trigger. My heart skipped a beat. By the grace of God the gun didn't go off. The boy was surprised. Then he took the gun away from my head and put the gun in the air and the gun went off. I gave them the money and ran to my cousin's house to tell him what happened.

My parents called the police and I explained to them what happened and I also told them the person's name. The white officer told me since he didn't witness the act; he could not arrest the person. He told me it's my word against his word, and he will make a report. I guess since it was a black on black crime it didn't matter that much. Those guys could have killed me and the police would just make a report and take no action at all. After these two incidents with the police, I made up my mind to never trust anyone wearing a police uniform.

I recall a happy moment in my life when I cleared the eighth grade. I went back to let the nun know about this. Instead of appreciating me, she said that it was sheer luck that I graduated and also stated that I would not graduate high school.

My ninth grade year I confronted the nun, because I kept wondering why a person of God would keep saying all of these negative things about me. The nun told me she never told me any of those things and I must have made them up in my head. At that time the nun must have been around 90 years old.

My ninth grade year I went to Marquette High School. Most of my classmates were children that I knew from the other private schools. They were smart and could also read well. We played sports together. Our classes were pretty small; around 25-40 students.

Attending the religion class was mandatory. We had a young person who was probably two or three years into priesthood as our teacher. He seemed to be a student favorite. I remember many times in class I would raise my hand to read and he wouldn't call on me at all. The young priest would point out everything I was doing wrong and nothing I was doing right.

I remember one time in class during the Iran Contra, one of the students raised their hand and asked the priest as to why the black people were sent home first. The young priest told the student, "Black people are not worth anything; they drive around in their Cadillac and live off the government."

The student then asked the priest, "What about John and Dion?" The young priest quickly replied, "Well, they are a different type of black populace."

At this time, the priest planted a seed that black people are not worth anything, so the 25-45 children in the room believed what he stated because he had the authority.

I went home to tell my mother about what the priest mentioned in the class. My mother made an appointment with the school principal and the priest. We met about three days later. When we arrived, we all sat down. I spoke first to explain what took place. After I spoke, the young priest agreed to whatever I had stated and he also explained even more. The principal then took up for the young priest. At this point my mother told the school if that was how they see black people, that her son would be leaving the school. It seemed like they really didn't care. My mother seemed very upset since most of her children attended Marquette and this was the way they were treating us after many years of dedication to the school. My mother decided to get me admitted to a different school.

The following year I went to Elston High School. Compared to Marquette, it was night and day. I remember my first day for college prep courses. I arrived to class and the teacher asked if I was in the right class. I inquired if this was the Chemistry class and he nodded. He again stated that I must be in the wrong class and that the shop class was down the hall. I told him that I am very much in the right class. The teacher had me go to a counselor just to make sure if I am in the right class. Going to Elston made me understand how to be black in America. Going to Marquette High School they treated as I were a white person and or color didn't matter. At Elston High School I understood my place in the society/world.

I really felt it was a blessing to go to Elston as it made me face reality about who I was and about life. Elston, at first seemed very hard for me. The teens were very rude and mean. They were always talking trash, which was something I didn't get at Marquette. I had the honor of being able to be a part of both worlds. I grew up with all my friends from St Mary's, and after going to Elston, people would see me as being a black person whereas at Marquette we were in a fantasy world and we thought we were the same as the white children until reality kicked in. I have always believed that everything happens for a reason and a purpose in life, and I am happy for going to Elston as I really met some good lifetime friends at both schools.

The nun died while I was at my tenth grade year. It was a bitter sweet feeling that I had and more than anything I was saddened that she died before I could prove her wrong. Though she was not at her best behavior with me, she had helped so many people along her career.

As you realize, I had many seeds planted in my life before turning 16 years old. I view my seeds as a blessings because I always had the most powerful seed. My father told me I had to be 100 times smarter than everyone else and so I worked very hard by studying and doing my best. He also told me that he had only received a third grade education and all of his children would go to college because the more you learn, the more you will earn. My mother would always call me handsome and would always say that I would be someone of great influence. Both of my parents constantly planted positive seeds in my garden. The world would plant seeds as well. I had a choice to believe the world or my parents, and I am so happy I chose to believe my parents most of the time.

People would always tell me "sticks and stone may break your bones but words will never hurt."

This statement is false. I would rather have someone beat me up instead of have someone hurt me with their words. Wounds will heal with time, but if someone plants negative seeds in your life, you will think about it, visualize it and then will manifest the negative statement or phrase the person told you. Eventually you will end up believing it.

I did graduate high school and I praise God for that. I beat what the nun told me. I still had this label about who I was stuck in my mind though. In the back of my head the seeds the nun planted for me I sometimes watered, put on sunshine, and asked myself if I was really retarded.

I remember when I was 31 years old, I had a career in the mental health field and I still had those negative seeds planted from the nun. I still had a question of who I was. I remember reading excerpts from this book called Unlimited Power by Anthony Robbins. This book changed my life. I would use some of the same techniques from the book at my job.

At that time I was working at River Edge Hospital in Forest Park, Illinois. I helped my mentor; Carl Scott, open up the first Residential Treatment center for adolescents.

I found out that Anthony Robbins would be in Chicago for a one day sales seminar. The ticket was priced at $297.00. This happened in the year 1995. I went to the seminar and this one day event changed my life. After the seminar I wanted to be on stage helping people. I wanted to be the next Anthony Robbins. I remember that I told some of my close friends about my experience.

They would discourage me by saying "Who would pay to listen to you? You stutter!" I took those words as a challenge. I told myself that I was not in first grade anymore. I will dictate my own future by planting positive seeds.

Anthony Robbins had a second seminar coming in the Chicago land area in July of 1995 called Unleash the Power. A four day program would cost $695.00. This was equal to my two weeks of pay, way back in the year 1995. I did not think much and attended the seminar. What he taught me changed my life forever. He planted so many positive seeds in my life. For the first time I was around liked minded people who were dealing with some of the same challenges and having the right tools and strategies to overcome them. At the seminar, I changed my meaning of my stutter problem. I viewed it in a different way, which changed my destiny.

At that seminar I met Joseph McClendon III, a head trainer of Anthony's organization and he taught me a breathing technique that changed the way I spoke forever. I didn't label myself as a stutter anymore. I told the world I that am a genius and sometimes I might stumble across my words because I have to take more time to choose the right one. At times I see Anthony Robbins stutter, so I know that I am in good company. Being a genius was something that I was OK with. Taking on this meaning really changed my life forever.

From the bottom of my heart, I thank Anthony Robbins and my mentor Joseph McClendon III for giving me the tools I needed to change my life and all the privileges I have had to be a part of changing other people's lives.

I know without a doubt that the seeds that Tony Robbins and Joseph McClendon III planted stayed will with me for a life time, because I water them, and add fertilizer on them, and nourish them. I pulled out the weeds that were negative thoughts and I changed my environment. I had to be around like-minded people who had the same goals and dreams as I did. Your weeds will come up; meaning the seeds someone else has planted about you. When this takes place, pull up the weeds and replace them with something else which is positive. When I changed my environment, it really changed my life. I got around people who are living an incredible life in every area. So I have to play my A plus game to keep up with them.

Take a look at your own life right now. What seeds are you planting? When you talk about your problems, you are planting your seeds. When you are complaining, you are planting your seeds. When you are telling everyone your problems you are planting your seeds. Remember our thoughts, words and actions are creative, meaning that this is how we plant seeds in a negative way and in a positive way. What seeds are you planting today? Are you planting what someone told you about yourself or are you creating your own garden by living your dreams and goals by your own rules?

When I do reflect back on what my father mentioned so many times; that life is a garden and we dictate our life on a daily and weekly basis by what we hold in our mind and our thoughts.

I really believe the only thing that will make anything grow is having the right environment. Once we planted our garden we had to create the right environment in order to make it grow. I also believe that in order to make me grow to the person I am today I only have two people to thank. My parents. I really believe my parents planted their family in the right environment.

Power of an Environment

When you plant an acorn, 1000% of the time what comes up will be an Oak Tree. Why? Because of its environment. I really believe my parents put my siblings and myself in the right environment to grow. Let me explain why. My mother and father grew up as Baptists. My maternal grandfather was also from the Baptist ministry.

When my parents moved to Michigan City, Indiana, they wanted all their children to go to a private school and get the best education. In those days my parents had to be Catholic in order to do that, so they had to convert from Baptist to Catholic to create success and plant the right seed for their children.

The sacrifice my mother made is unimaginable. First she grew up as a Baptist, because her father (my grandfather) was a preacher. Then she turned into a devout

Catholic so that her children could get the best education and grow until the people my parents imagined they could be.

The reason for my success today is because of the environment in which I was brought up. I had the most amazing and supportive environment that was ready to help me grow. Looking back, it appears that my mother put the family in this environment to make us grow. Other children in our neighborhood went to public schools.

One of the best things about going to St Mary's as a child was that my parents and the parents of other children were so involved with the school. We had parents on the school grounds once we played outside, in the cafeteria and also on field trips with us.

Let me name a couple of parents I remember the most at St Mary's; we had Robby Bremer, Dion Campbell, Bob Gruse, Matt Rustboldt, Tim Greetham, Charlie Novak, Danny Black, Jeff Piper, Lucy Mazac, Paula Shultzs, Jennifer Darman, Tim Haas to name a few. We had more parents who came of course, but these are the parents and children who were very close and like family to me.

I really believe all the parents that I spent time with and the seeds they planted in my life reinforce everything that my parents told me. I can say that all the parents I spent time with planted powerful seeds and made me the man I am today. Given below is a short description about the people who made my environment successful.

My friend Robby Bremer's father worked at the Steel Mill. He was a protector, very direct, loyal and to the point. Robby's mother was very nice and kind. I would always hang out at Robby's house since we played in the same basketball team. I remember when I got my first car, Robby's father co-signed so I could get it.

Dion Campbell's father also worked at the Steel Mill. He was a preacher who talked about God. He was nice and very street smart. Dion's mother was very nice too. Like Robby, I would also spend a lot of time at

Dion's house because we also played basketball on the same team.

Matt Rustboldt's father was a businessman who owned the Shell Gas station. He was a very friendly person who always had a kind word to say. Matt's mother spent a lot of time on the playground with us. She was a lady with a warm heart; very nice and easy to speak with. I spent many days at Matt's house too. He was also part of the same basketball team. His father would always stop and talk to me once I visited the gas station.

I spent more time with Bob Gruse's mother, as his father worked a job. She was a very strong woman. Imagine this; she had to take care of six young men and she never missed a beat. She was very direct, nice and outgoing. All the boys knew that when Mrs. Gruse monitors the playground, no one could play rough at all. When she told us to jump, we all would ask how high!

Tim Greetham's father served time in the Military and then served a job. Mr. Greetham was more of a philosopher and was a very smart and good soul. Tim's mother was very nice and kind and would always talk with me. I would spend countless days playing with Tim; we would have sleep overs and his father would tell us so many stories about life.

Charlie Novak's mother spent a lot of time on the playground with us. She was very nice and didn't want us to ever play rough. Charlie's father taught at Marquette, the Catholic high school, so I never got to see him much.

Janet Retseck's father owned a shoe store and her mother was a teacher at St Mary's. I used to go to the shoe store all the time. I never had Mrs. Resteck as a teacher. I used to speak to both of them a lot.

Paul Gondeck's father served a job and his mother spent most of her time at the grade school. His mother was so nice and kind; always helpful to everyone. I would spend countless days hanging around and playing with Paul.

Paula Schultz's father was a Sales Engineer. His job involved designing for big car companies in Detroit. Her mother spent a lot of time in the school and going on trips. Both parents were nice and kind.

Jennifer Darman's father was a school principal and her mother worked at the bank. At St. Mary's we didn't have a school gym, so Mr. Darman rented out Mullins Elementary School to us. Mr. Darman was the coolest man, so down to earth, and always willing to help us out. Jenny's mother was nice and kind and easy to speak with.

Lucy Mazac's mother spent most of her time at the school, always giving 1000% helping all the students out. She was very friendly and outgoing. I remember when I came back to Michigan City in 2007 to do a book signing; Mrs. Mazac and Lucy were busy cheering me. It was a nice surprise!

Tim Haas's father owned a consulting engineer firm and his mother had to take care of their big family. I would see his mother come to the school often to help out. I spent many days at Tim's house and being around his nice parents. Since Tim and I played on the same basketball team, we had a strong bond of friendship.

Steve Palmer's father was the basketball coach. Mr. Palmer also owned an Upholstery Shop. I would often visit the shop and just talk to Mr. Palmer about life and basketball. Every time I came to his business, he would stop doing his work and speak to me.

Mike Johnson's father was also the basketball coach. He also worked at the local bank in the loan department. I used to come by to see Mr. Johnson and he would have on suits and ties. I told myself that when I grew up, I would be dressing the same way that he did.

Jerry Mitchell lived one block away from me. He lived with his grandfather Mr. Whitlow, who served a job. He had the best lawn in the neighborhood. Mr. Whitlow didn't take any mess and was a very smart guy. He always talked about respect and working hard. His wife was a very nice lady who had the prettiest roses for miles to come. From 1st grade to 8th grade, I spent most of my time with Jerry Mitchell. We did everything together once we got home from school.

Steve Upsher (Boo) also lived with his grandparents next door to our house. His grandfather would speak to me daily. I would always go to the store for him. His grandfather would always tell me that I slept too much. I don't think he knew that I used to wake up at 4:30 am and then go back to bed at 7:00 am in the summer time. His grandmother was also a nice and very talkative woman.

I met Steve Dabney for the first time during my 8th grade year. We played with his team during basketball and beat them. During my 10th grade year, I got transferred to Elston High School and Steve greeted me with open arms. We played together during my first year at the Elston.The best part about going to Elston was meeting his mother, Mary Dabney; I called her "Mrs. D." She was a strong woman with a heart of gold. Mrs. D would plant seeds in my garden like "don't listen to what people say and just play your game in basketball."

Coming from Marquette, our basketball style of play was totally different. At Elston, it was more of run and gun, always the same play but fast paced. We had a coach that I really didn't like. His name was Coach Steinke. I told Mrs. D that I just did not fit his style of play, so I quit the basketball team. Mrs. D seemed to be so upset. She would told me "Honey if you do not play, you will not be hurting anyone except yourself."

What true words she spoke. I have to say that was the last time in my life I quit because of what someone said about me. I didn't want to be known as a quitter and I didn't want one person to dictate future and give anyone that much power over me. Through the years, Mrs. D coached me on various things in my life and I would keep in contact with her at least once or twice a year. When I had my book signing in 2007 and my mother couldn't make it due to her health, Mrs. D came on behalf of my mother. She gave me the support I needed and continued to plant positive seeds in my life throughout the years. On May 2, 2012 she went to be with the Lord. I have to say what a huge loss it was to the world.

I met Steve Cabil at Elston High School. His stepfather and my father were good friends. I lived at his house and vice versa. His mother was nice and kind and could cook very well. You always remember good food!

During grade school as well as high school, I would hang out with many people. I really believed the environment my parents put me around made me succeed. All of my friends were successful too. When I was younger, I would see my sisters and brothers all go to college and even graduate. So when my father told me I was going to college, I knew it was possible because of the seeds he had previously planted with my other siblings.

I also knew I had to be a success in life because of my environment. Each parent in my childhood who affected my life, contribute towards my success. I really believed each of them and I took on their personality and they enforced what my parents told me about the world.

Mr. Bremer: I took his kind heart and his directness.

Mrs. Dabney: Her never give up attitude and always striving to be your best.

Mr. Campbell: Putting God first. Most of my programs are spiritual based.

Mr. Rustboldt: He was a businessman and now I own my own companies.

Mrs. Gruse: To stand up for myself and to be independent.

Mr.Greetham: He was a philosopher. I have a PhD in Philosophy.

Mr. Darman: He was down to earth and very cool guy; I guess he planted great seeds because I am down to earth and a cool guy too.

Mr. Haas: He was a businessman, very nice and serious at times. I see the same qualities in myself.

Mr. Palmer: Definitely the coach and the business man. I provide business coaching and own companies.

Mr. Johnson: Another coach and a sharp dresser. When I see my clients or speak at an event I dress to impress.

Mr. Schultz: This guy was the super sales person. Any business owner is a sales person. I am an expert in sales.

Mr. Whitlow: His work ethic, directness, and walking his talk. I picked up many fine points from Mr. Whitlow.

Mrs. Mazac: She was so nice and kind and very helpful to everyone who gave 1000% every time. I picked up all the seeds Mrs. Mazac planted in my life.

All of these parents as well as the young people who I hung around with in my life contributed towards my success. As I mentioned earlier, once you plant an acorn, 1000% of the time an oak tree comes up. When my parents planted me at St. Mary's and by the grace of God, my environment pulled me in the right direction in my life.

POINTS TO PIN DOWN:

Like John Oda, a young man with many negative seeds being planted before the age of 16, what dreams and goals are you not pursuing just because someone talked you out of your dreams? As you know, whatever seed you plant (negative and or positive) it will grow. What seeds are you planting on a daily basis? Here are some questions to think about before you go to the next chapter.

1. What did you learn from my story?

2. What seeds are you planting right now?

3. Are you planting bad seeds like complaining, blaming other people, not taking responsibility for your actions?

4. What positive seeds are you planting on a daily basis?

5. What stories are you telling yourself which makes you drive in neutral in your life?

6. What new positive seeds are you going to plant today?

Chapter 1: Have Faith

"And Jesus answering saith unto them; have faith God!

For verily I say unto you. That whosoever shall say unto this mountain, Be thou removed and be thou cast into the sea, and shall not doubt in his heart, but shall believe that those things which he saith shall come to pass, he shall have whatsoever he saith. Therefore I say unto you. What thingssoever ye desire when ye pray, believe that ye receive them, and ye shall have them." **Mark 11:22-24**

What is faith? Faith is something that you cannot see. It is invisible, but when I really saw faith and the way it applied to me in my life, it was simply magical. My father and I would plough the garden and do everything we needed to do in order to prepare it properly. Then, my father would plant the seeds.

I would say, "Dad, how do you know these seeds would grow?

He said, "Baby, you got to have faith!"

He said, "Baby, if you put sunshine, water, lime and fertilizer, they will grow."

Then, I realized the same thing can be applied in our life. What is faith? If you speak about it, if you talk about it, if you change your thoughts, if you focus on the positives, if you do the action, it will happen because you have faith.

Another thing about faith is that my father had an expectation. He had a knowing that his garden would grow. Not a hope, not a wish; because if you hope, you move your body differently. If you wish, it's like rolling the dice. If you have that expectation then no matter what, it's going to happen.

My father knew that when he planted those seeds in the garden, when he planted the greens, the tomatoes, the cucumbers, the green beans, the collards, the mustards, he knew that they would grow. He had a knowing. He had an expectation.

Biblically speaking, when Jesus performed the miracle, what he said was that God told him and he said, "Thank you, Father."

When he said, "Thank you, Father," when people had leprosy, which is AIDS today, he didn't say, "I hope I can heal them." He didn't say, "I wish I could heal them." No, he had an expectation. He had a knowing. With the knowing, He did it without a doubt. It was done already.

Do you have an expectation for your goals and dreams? We can have an expectation in a positive and an expectation in a negative. It depends on the environment in which we hang out. For instance, when my father had the garden, he had an environment. When he planted the mustard greens, we knew that ten times out of ten that it was going to grow to become mustard green. The mustard green didn't turn out to be collard greens or green

3

beans; it simply came out as mustard greens. Why? It was because of the environment.

How is your environment? Whatever your environment is, it dictates your life tremendously. When you have the sunshine on the plant, when you have time to get rid of the bugs, when you have fertilizer, when you water it, when the weeds come up and also when you pull out the weeds, you care caring for the environment. If you don't pull out the weeds from your garden, the plant will die. Similarly, you need to pull out the weeds existing inside your life: negative thinking, anger, stress, worry and fear. You should also avoid mingling with people who are naysayers, who don't believe in you, and are negative. It will do you no good being in their company.

People have a fear of criticism because if they tell others and they don't really believe what was told, they have a fear to tell anyone that they may cross paths with. They have a fear of being criticized. People will talk about them. My dad would always say to keep loving people who talk about you. My theory is that you should not care or worry about people who talk about you. My dad once told me when I was small that people do not pay for your rent. People do not give you any money. People don't make your bowels move. Who cares what they think? But you got to have faith. You have to have faith in yourself: Faith and expectation. Faith like a mustard seed and you must have faith in God or your higher power.

One day, I was thinking about my dad when he planted the garden. He put on fertilizer. Not sure if you know this, but fertilizer stinks.

I said, "Dad, why do you put on fertilizer? It stinks!"

Dad said, "Son, if you put fertilizer on, it's going to make the plant grow."

"But dad, its manure! It stinks! You're making the whole garden stink."

"Baby, you put fertilizer on, it's going to make it grow."

I thought about that. He was right. Every time he puts fertilizer on the garden, the plant would grow; why? Because of nutrients, because of what it needed, it was in the right environment and it grew. At times in our life, we get fertilizer put on us and it stinks. It's like going through turbulence and it hurts. We need to overcome it. This is because the fertilizers we get put on our lives, they make us grow, make us stronger, and make us realize our true potential.

In my life, if I really think back, I've been dealing with a lot fertilizer in my life all the time. Every time that God put fertilizer on me, it would stink. I realized that I had to go through the situation. Things turned bad and it made me grow. It made me grow in every area; my confidence, my financials and my relationships. I also had to grow in my self-confidence as well.

The same thing that we do for our plants, God does for us. The reason why I really believe this is because the concept is that we have to grow. When you get these bad breaks and everything else is going wrong, just realize right now that God just put that in front of you. You must have faith in your higher power. You have to know that whatever takes place, you can surely get out of it.

Have you ever been on an airplane? When on an airplane, there are times when you get that turbulence and the plane is shaking. You're like, "Oh my God, I'm going to die," but eventually it stops and everything is okay 99.0% of the time. One percent, things might not be okay.

The same thing happens in our life. To me, when I go through a bad phase, I welcome it because I know that I'm going to grow. When you face trouble in your relationship, in your finances, in whatever area of your life, you're going to grow without a doubt. When tough times come down hard on me, instead of fighting it, I remind myself to "dance with my problems," meaning I know I will grow in every way so I welcome the growth.

Let me explain to you how I applied faith in my mental health business. I've done that for 23 years and really enjoy it.

Case study number five. It's in my book called *Connecting with Your Teen: The 7 Principles to Resolve Teenage Behavior Challenges.*

I worked with a kid there. This kid was one of the worst kids that the state of Oregon ever had. They never thought he was going to actually amount to anything. His father hated women and that's what he taught his child as a kid. The man would ill-treat his wife and the kid would see this.

His parents sent him to a different country. People used to beat him up, spank him, and put him in closets. When the kid came back home, I met him. He was about 11 years old. He was buck wild and out of control.

His parents gave me this big list of what this kid had wrong with him and also came to a conclusion that this kid was never going to change.

I said, "We will see."

I talked to him. Let's call the kid Robert just for name's sake.

I said, "Robert, you know," I looked at him. "Listen to me. These people know so much and they really want to help you out so much. Probably it's all wrong. I believe that without a doubt, you can graduate college, you can graduate high school, and you can do whatever that you choose to."

I planted a seed in his life and I really believed in what I told him. I planted a seed in him. A seed was a possibility that he could make a complete change in his life. Without a doubt, I knew he could. However, he set the wrong strategy.

So I further worked with this kid, literally, for maybe three months. I had private sessions with him, family sessions, group family sessions; whatever it took to make a complete change. The kid graduated high school with a 3.1 grade point average. No one even thought he would graduate high school.

In his high school years, he definitely had some turbulence. He got addicted to drugs and was smoking marijuana and doing crazy things that kids do.

He went to college at the University of Oregon. I remember during his freshmen year, he said, "Dr. John, I need your help. Could you come up with a time management system so I can enjoy school as well as do whatever it takes?" I created one for him and with the grace of God, the kid graduated in four years with a double major.

Robert went to the Navy for four years. Now he's flying helicopters. It was a seed that I planted. I watered and put fertilizer on the seed. I gave Robert sunshine and hope. I do know we must plant the right seeds in our own lives in the same manner.

I had this one business that I loved to death. I still work with this client today. In two years, we made $300,000! I followed the same principles that my father taught me: in the garden as well as in the business. Two years later, our business grew up to $2.8 million. In

2015 we should do $7-8 million dollars in business.

How did I make changes so quickly? I planted the seed to push them beyond their thinking. I gave them a game plan and I had them do incantations. You will learn more about this in the next chapter on Mindset. At this point the company has a new expectation. Again, I planted the right seeds; I helped them add fertilizer and sunshine. We planted many seeds we didn't know which ones would grow up. The only one we had was faith.

I had them tap into the seed of their higher power, because I am just a vessel that believes in my higher power and we used some powerful business techniques which we will cover in the chapter on strategy.

My clients now have faith in themselves and find ways to tap into their higher power by creating an expectation about the way they see their business and use the same principles to grow their company now. As I believe in my higher power, I know I can accomplish anything through Him.

I will show you ways on how to create the same results in every area of your life. In this book you will learn how we created 900% in my client's company. Once you read the chapter on strategy, time management and passion, you will see how using this book, we can transform all areas of *your* life as well.

As a part of this new way of thinking, I will show you how to create a knowing. I don't care if it rains on your parade. I don't care if people say that you can't do it. Who cares?

My outcome is to create the results you must have in your life and the only thing you must do is put in the work now. As you know, tomorrow never comes and the only thing we have is **NOW**.

The same thing that we do for our plant, God does for us. The reason why I really believe this is because the concept is that we have to grow. When we get these bad breaks and everything else, just realize right now that God just put a challenge in front of you. You have to have faith in your higher power. You have to know that whatever takes place; you can and will get out of it.

We have all used expectation in our lives. I know when I bought my first brand new car; I would tell whoever would listen to me about how nice it was. I would read books and go to the car place several times. I had this expectation; I would work long hours, and grab all the overtime I could because I knew I had this car. I would think about it and see myself driving in my dream car. I could hear the engine of my Nissan Maxima. Three months later, I received my peal white, tan interior, new car. Now it's your turn: write down your last goals and dreams. Now write down one thing you have to accomplish, like buying a house, car, going to college and please tell me the steps you will take to make it happen. I believe you probably will do the same thing everyone did to accomplish their goal or dream.

POINTS TO PIN DOWN:

By now your realize faith is the key to attain massive success in your life. Faith with the proper application and instruction will help feed the subconscious mind to reach amazing success. In the story, my father had so much faith in his garden that we would speak things in existence and have a knowing his garden will grow all the time.

Here are few questions you need to answer before going to the next chapter.

1. What fertilizer is now making you grow in your life?

2. What was once a dream and now you have accomplished in your life (Car, house, going to college)? How did you get it? Write down the steps.

3. What is the perfect environment you can live in your life right now? To reach your goals and dreams paint me a picture of your perfect environment.

4. How do you define expectation? Are you expecting good and bad things to happen in your life? Make a list on a weekly basis on how many good and bad things you expect in your life.

5. How do you define faith? In what areas in your life are you activating your faith?

6. Are you activating your faith in a negative way?

7. What areas in your life do you need to speak in existence so you can activate your faith?

"Both poverty and riches are the offspring of success." -Think and Grow Rich

Chapter 2: Mindset

"Set your mind on the higher things and keep it set." Colossian's 3:2

My dad had a mind-set that you wouldn't believe. He renewed his mind on a daily basis. Every time I would talk to my dad, even in the last years of his life, I knew he was not doing the greatest. I would say, "Baby, how are you doing!"

He said, "I'm doing a hundred." His mind set was so amazing, so incredible. Even while working on the garden, his mind set was incredible.

I remember times being together in Michigan City, Indiana. We had snow storms. He planted the garden despite of it snowing. Two weeks later, it killed his whole garden. He reassured me by saying, "Baby, don't worry about it. We'll get the greens. Everything will come up again." It did.

The concept is with a mind-set, you can choose to be happy or you can choose to be sad. It's a choice. What you choose to be is up to you. Watching my dad and his garden, he chose to be in a positive mind set. Nothing would shake him. They used to call him the Batman because the Batman would make a way out of no way, and he did, each and every time.

Having ten children, he sent us all to private schools. That's a mind-set. This mind-set that he actually had, (one mind-set that he actually had though) I really appreciate it. He had a mind-set of his father, of God. My father believed in God. He might not have gone to church every Sunday like most people would, but he believed in God.

I think he gave his tithe from his garden. People would come by and dad would give them food. If people would come by there, he would give greens or tomatoes, whatever. He had the habit of giving unconditionally. He didn't charge or try to do a business. He just gave it away.

He had the mindset of trusting in God. He was thanking God in advance. He had this expectation to know that things will actually take place.

I do what I call incantations. Incantations can be a statement or a phrase. I got this from *Think and Grow Rich,* chapter four, Auto Suggestion. I say this with feelings, and emotions, until it gets into my subconscious mind, until it becomes my incantations, so I will incant something that's positive.

I will give you an example to depict the reason why I always tell my clients to say incantations. As you know, I worked in the mental health field for over 23 years. When I would meet teenagers, I would ask them what positive things their parents would say about them, and they would give me a list of maybe 2-3 things. Then I would ask them what are the negative things, and they would give me a list of 8-20 things. I would then ask them how their parents would tell these negative statements to them. About 99% would say with feelings and emotions. One of my teens told me his mother told him he would be like his father, who is in jail right now. His mother would say it with feeling and emotions at least 10-15 times per week. As you probably realize, her son went to jail because his mother used an incantation in the reverse way.

I remember as a child my mother used to tell me how handsome I am, and believe me back then I felt like an ugly duckling! I had acne all over my face, and I really didn't look and or feel handsome at all. My mother would say this so much, with feeling and emotions she made me believe it, and today I tell the entire world how handsome and smart I am. Thanks Mommy "O" for planting powerful seeds in my life.

I once went to a seminar of Tony Robbins. He mentioned that he made $3,000.00 per month, and in 9 months he made one million dollars. Then he mentioned that he used incantations to create a shift in his thinking, and this changed his life forever.

When I went to Anthony Robbins' seminars, this is one of his incantations he would use *"God's wealth is circulating in my life. His wealth flows to me in avalanches of abundance. All my needs, desire and goals are met instantaneously by infinite intelligence for I am one with God and God is everything."*

I did some investigation on incantations and how I can apply them in my life. I read a wonderful book called *Think and Grow Rich* by Napoleon Hill, a classic in the personal development field. For the last 15 years I read this book every three months. Napoleon Hill writes a chapter called Autosuggestion. It mentions that if you say a statement with feelings and emotions until it gets in the subconscious mind, things will change. He also mentioned that people like Henry Ford, John D Rockefeller, Woodrow Wilson, Thomas Edison, and Theodore Roosevelt used the same principles.

I did more research on these incantations. I read one of the Pastor Joel Osteen books. Pastor Joel was based out of Houston. He mentioned that when he took over his father's church, he started using the same principles and this changed his life forever. Pastor Joel Osteen said that this is how he created success in his life by doing this for 15 to 30 minutes per day.

He would incant, "I am blessed. The favor of God has turned my situation around. God is opening doors of opportunity ""The favor of God is following me, I am the head not the tail, I am the lender not the borrower, something good is going to happen."

I took all these information from all these sources I gathered over the years. Then I used my last source. I read the Bible. The Bible mentions that you must renew your mind on a daily basis. I asked myself as to what this actually meant.

After looking at all the people I respect, I realized that I needed to take some action in my own life. What if I would say a positive statement with feelings and emotions? Would this change my life and make me have faith? I had to find out, so I tried saying my incantations, autosuggestion or affirmation on steroids.

I've tried them in my own life and it did change every area of my life. It changed my finance, my confidence level, my speaking, and my weight loss. In every area I changed. I've tried the same concept on one of my business clients; he appeared to be the most negative person I've met in a long time. He just didn't believe that I could help him grow his business.

I told my client to read *Think and Grow Rich*, and then we talked about faith. One of the ways to get faith would be to start saying incantations. My client told me that he agreed on doing so. We had a weekly session. After 2 weeks, I asked him how his business was. He told me with the same old negative attitude that it was the same as he had two weeks ago. I asked him if he was saying his incantations with feelings and emotions and for at least to start 10 minutes per day. He said, "Well not really, maybe one time." I explained to him the reason why he was producing the same results in his life.

The next week one of his employees quit. At first he thought this must have been the worst thing that could take place but in reality it was the best thing because he had to drive the truck for 8-10 hours per day. My client started saying his incantations in the truck with feelings and emotions. After the first week he had some pep in his step. It seemed like he was having more faith and taking more actions on his business. In less than 8 months the net profit grew to 120% and he started having record breaking weeks. He would double the weeks in production, in some weeks he would break the bank. His business grew so much that he had to buy another truck and also hire three more people!

Now imagine everything what took place was when there was a very hard recession. In 18 months, even with the added expenses meaning the truck and hiring new people, his net profit grew. He bought a dream house that was over 20,000 square feet. Now he says his incantations last around 60-90 minutes per day. The last time I spoke to him, we implemented profit stations to grow his business and now he is seeing a 400% increase in his net profit. My client's faith is so strong now that he can even move mountains. It's amazing to see the growth he made in his life in less than eight months. Every area of his life has changed. I am so proud I could help in his growth and in having faith.

A reason to renew your mind every day is because we want to rid ourselves of our negative thinking and negative thoughts. I believe we all have what I call a different vibration. Let me give you an example. If you take water and freeze it becomes ice/snow. You take the same water and boil it, what happens is that it becomes steam. It is the same water that changes as per the circumstances.

Once we are having negative emotions, we are in a different vibration. For example: anger, worry, stress, fear, financial and health problems. We move our body differently, we are moving slower and most people are not at his or her best. Now when you are in a higher vibration like, being cheerful, passionate, excited, grateful and happy, you get the point. When you are in the higher vibration, you look at the world in a different way, your body language is totally different, the way you talk is different and what you believe is different. When I was growing up, we used to have a VFH and a UFH. We had different channels and on certain stations you could see more clearly. I really believe when some people are in a lower vibration like depression, anger, worry; they tap into all of the radio stations and or mindset who are on this station. So what I tell people is if you are on a lower vibration you are in slavery, because now you are thinking about it, you are talking about it and ultimately you are becoming your problem. You are tapping into the same radio station as all the negative people are around you.

I will take it one step further. I worked in the mental health field for 23 years; I had the honor of helping people out with many issues. What I did find out was that most people are in a lower vibration like stress, worry, depression, fear, and when this takes place they tap into the radio stations of all these people. What take place is that they are in such a low vibration that they have suicidal thoughts; they sometimes try to kill themselves. I always ask myself why, and I really believe they tap into other people's radio stations, and thereby create his or her own mental slavery.

I believe if you hold a negative thought like, anger, stress, worry, not forgiving a person, guilt, health problems, financial problems; you are in slavery. The reason why is because it will be your focus each and every day. If you don't know how to forgive people you are in slavery and you are in bondage; you have the chains around you.

Whatever you will focus on you will feel. If you have financial problems, health issues, worry stress, fear; you are in slavery. Take a moment to reflect to see if you are in bondage with the above examples. Most people only focus on the negative emotions, so they are planting seeds in the reverse way. Now they are planting worry, stress, health issues, money problems, they are giving it attention, they are adding the sunshine, and they are talking about it with their family and friends. You will complain about it, you will talk about it and then you will end up being one. Every time you talk about it, you are planting more seeds; most people add too much fertilizer and wonder why there life is so messed up and why their garden won't grow.

Your body is not supposed to have the fear, worry, doubt and stress. I want to have you do an exercise for me. Take out a piece of paper; write down your fear, worry, stress, anger; whatever issues you face right now. Then get a glass of water and fill it ¾th. Take the piece of paper with all your statements on it. Then crunch it and place it in the water, and let it sit there for 5 minutes.

Now I want you to take the paper out. How does it look? Messed up? The paper is probably falling apart at this point and it probably feels gross. I believe that when you have stress, worry, doubt, fear, and anger, the body reacts the same way. Your body is not meant for people to be in slavery. I know there are people who are angry over something that happened 20 years ago. When this takes place, our body is out of balance and this is how we get diseases.

This is only my option right now. I really believe this is why people get cancer, arthritis, because they hold in all these emotions and they can't forgive people. I also believe some diseases do come from your genetics. When you are stressed out, the weak link will break. I have personally experienced it in my own life. I used to live in the State of Washington, and I found out my father got sick so I moved back to Fisher Indiana. I forgot about the weather back in Indiana, so when we moved at first, my wife Keiko liked Indiana, but after the winter time she didn't like it so much. The spring approached and one day we had a tornado watch, again I forgot about how bad the weather could be because I had not been back home in years. We moved back right around the same time Japan had their big earthquake, Tsunami, and the nuclear reactor went crazy. I went on a trip to Dubai and I forgot when we have a tornado that the sirens come on but when the tornados leave; this is when you don't hear them.

Once I left, we had a severe tornado. The town about 60 miles from us just got wiped out and the tornado appeared to be coming our way. My wife heard those sirens and freaked out. When I got back home from Dubai she was in the bathroom crying. I asked her how long she had been in the bathroom for. She just couldn't recollect. I found out that the tornado left two days prior. The next day my wife wanted to move. I told my wife we just couldn't move because we had only been there for barely six months. Every time we would watch the news and they mention a tornado warning, my wife would stress out and almost have a panic attack. In the three years we stayed in Indiana she had bronchitis, shingles in her 30's, a gall stone and gall bladder surgery! (Surprisingly my wife is such a healthy eater!)

I really believed she had all these problems due to her stress. Once we moved from Fisher, Indiana to Irvine, California, she has not got sick in the last two years. She's happier, her health is so much better because she changed and got out of a stressful environment and away from the tornados.

I was told another story about a hardworking man. He worked at the railroad and everyone said he was the most negative person on earth. One day he worked late, and he went into a freezer and the door closed behind him. He yelled and screamed, pleading for help but nobody could hear him at all. He started getting nervous and tensed.

His negativity kicked in. He told himself how cold he was and how he would be dying soon. The temperature gauge broke and read 40 degrees but after sometime it was actually 68 degrees in the freezer. The man had so much negativity that he wrote a note, telling people he would die now. He wrote his family a letter talking about how cold he felt. The next morning they found him dead as he believed he was freezing even though his temperature was not below normal. This is what I mean. Your body is not supposed to have the fear, worry, doubt, non-forgiveness and or any negative emotions or they will find a way to manifest.

I remember reading about the mindset in the Bible. It had a story about the widow woman. In 1 Kings 17:7-28 Elijah came to the widow woman and he knocked on the door. The old widow says, "Listen to me; I have only a little cornmeal. After this cornmeal, my sons and I are going to die."

He says, "Oh no, no, no. That's not going to happen like that. You feed the men of God first," He also adds, "Do me a favor. Go to your neighbor's and get me some barrels. Don't get one, but get as many barrels as you choose to." She came back with six barrels. After this, he changed her mindset and those six barrels lasted for two to three years!

If you look at all the stories in the Bible, they talk about changing your mind set, changing your focus, and changing your vibration.

You have to change your vibration when you say your incantations too. When you change your mindset, you're changing your vibrations as a whole. When this take place I believe miracles happen, because now you are in the spirit.

Now, think about it. When you are in the spirit, you're really in that state of expectancy then it happens. When you are praying, and when you pray with a negative thought or a negative statement, or a negative incantation, it's not going to happen again, this won't take place. You pray for one thing, but your words, your thoughts, and your actions are totally different. Again, it's all about the mindset. Just like my father had the mindset every year that his garden would grow and he would feed his children and the neighborhood and it did. To me, mindset is everything. When you have the proper mindset your whole world changes.

POINTS TO PIN DOWN:

When saying your incantations to create wealth or something positive, the words spoken with feeling and emotions reach the subconscious mind. Once this is done on a consistent basis, like 15 to 90 per day with feelings and emotions, it will get you one step closer towards your goals and dreams and rid you from poverty.

When you can imagine and feel, and see whatever you are creating in your life like money, this will activate a new money conscious which will create more wealth in your life. After you start doing your incantations, you will find ways to improve your business by a hunch or a feeling. Act on this new way of thinking now. Waiting for the right time is the number one cause of defeat in any calling.

Here are few questions you need to answer before moving to the next chapter.

1. How many negative emotions do you feel per week? Please write down the

emotions (Example: fear, worry, stress, anger, non-forgiveness)

2. How many positive emotions do you feel per week? (Example: cheerfulness, happy, passion, excitement)

3. What negative emotions are you planting per week?

4. What are you new incantations you will say with feeling and emotions to create success in your life?

5. What challenges are you facing now? How can you "dance with your fertilizer?"

6. Create a journal of the challenges you are facing and write down what you are learning from these challenges.

7. Write down your new incantation.

Chapter 3: Strategy

Strategy: A strategy is a plan of action or policy designed to achieve a major or overall aim. It is the art of planning, grand design, game plan (of action) action plan, policy or program. For example: a military operation and movement during a war or battle.

When I hear the definition of strategy, it makes me think of when my father had his beloved garden. My father had a clear strategy.

Dad always said, "Baby, you can't reap and sow in the same season."

When my father told me that last statement, I asked him what it meant. He explained that when you plant a seed, you cannot eat the fruit or vegetable the same day. You have to wait some time before you can eat the food in the garden.

First, daddy would plant his garden, always right before Easter. It was somewhere between the end of April and early May. Maybe sometimes it was early April. It depends on when Easter is every year. So before this time, my brother and I would have to clean out the garden from last year. Like I told you in the beginning of the book, we would have to dig up the garden and pull out the collard greens stalks. We would have to clean out the trash from the previous year as well as what came in from the hard winter storms. This process would take some time to get the garden ready for my father to plant.

I would ask for help from the neighborhood children because this garden, at that time appeared to be so big and huge especially in the eyes of a child. My father had a strategy for my brother and me and he told us what he wanted us to do and he also gave us a time table to get it done.

One day my brother Ben had a great game plan. My father wanted us to dig out the garden, so my brother suggested that we only dig out every three feet and tell our dad that we dug out the entire garden. My brother told me our father is old and so he would not understand. At the time my father was only 53 years old. The next morning, my father woke up my brother and me at 4:00 am in the morning telling us we didn't do the garden the right way. The colorful language which came from his mouth clearly indicated that this time my brother and I had messed up. My father made us do it the right way at 4am. This was the last time I listened to my brother's great game plans!

My father and his friends would till the garden several times because the ground was still cold. They would do this process about two or three times before they would plant any seeds. As a child, I would watch this process because most of the neighborhood children would be doing the same process if their fathers owned a garden.

On Good Friday, he started planting his garden. My father would plant a lot of mustard greens first because of the time of the year. When you first walk out to the garden he would plant maybe five to eight roles of mustard greens. My father had his own little strategy of what to plant first based on the weather. It appeared almost like he had a map in his own head. I really believed he got his strategy by modelling his grandfather when he lived in Mississippi.

My father lived on a farm growing up and now I really believe he took what he learned and applied it to his garden in Michigan City, Indiana. Watching my father in his garden was like poetry in motion.

My father would always 100% of the time start off planting the mustard greens. He wouldn't plant the tomatoes until I think June due to the weather. He would plant the okra though. I think his game was to plant what could bear the unpredictable weather in the month of April/May.

I could see the garden in front of me because I know what he had planted. He would plant about one to eight rows of mustard greens. He would have my brother and me water it and put lime on it so the bugs wouldn't eat the plants. He would also ask us to water the garden daily at certain times of the day, early in the morning or late at night.

My dad would say, "Baby, in two weeks, we're going to be ready to eat these."

Of course I couldn't see it, but I guess he did. My father had the vision and I could only see what was in front of me at the time. I took what my father taught me as a child with having the right strategy and applied this in every area of my life.

About four years ago, I gained a lot of weight; maybe close to 100 pounds. At that time my father was still alive. I came up with a strategy to shed off the extra pounds. At one time I weighed 245 pounds and I took some growth hormones to get leaner. I didn't know that you weren't supposed to eat any fattening foods. I ended up weighing close to 335 pounds in less than nine months! I went to several doctors and they didn't know what actually took place. I still worked out six times per day, doing group classes, jogging, and doing everything, however the weight came and stayed.

I told myself that if I didn't get a hold of my weight I was going to be close to 500 pounds. So I had to create a strategy to lose this weight. I had to give a speech in New York at that time. A very close friend told me that I looked like a fat pig and I deserved more than what I was doing right now. Those words hurt, and the sad thing was that my friend told me the truth. I really believe that a true friend will tell you the truth all the time. At that point I didn't have enough pain to make a change. I added on another six months and 60 pounds before I took any action to create a game plan.

I went to Japan in 2011 to attend the wedding of my sister in law. At that time I only weighed 295 pounds. I stayed in Japan and gained over 25 pounds in three weeks. I ate anything in my sight, because I told myself that I was on a vacation. What a crazy excuse!

When I got home from Japan, I hit rock bottom because I knew I am not living the way I should be living. I knew that I could do better. I realized that I needed a strategy to get this weight off. So I gave myself one year to shed the weight off and keep it off.

I started this eating plan one week before Christmas. I took away all the junk food and candy. I stopped eating rice and energy rich food for the first 90 days. I only ate less than 1500 calories per day and at the gym I must have burned off 1000 plus. I visualized the new me on a daily basis, and in 90 days I lost 75 pounds and 75 inches off my body. I have kept the weight off for the last three years. I have a similar eating program now. I work out six to seven days per week, and eat about 80-90% clean.

I realized that working with business required a strategy, I have found out when you focus on education and being the expert in your field, you get more respect. Nobody wants to be sold, everyone wants to be educated. When I took on this new way of thinking, my companies exploded in business. I also focused on finding the low hanging fruit, meaning that I learned how I was going to make the most money now. I have found out that most business people are tacticians, meaning they have a website, business plan and do some marketing and the goal is to educate.

Reflecting back to my father, he always had a strategy when planting a garden and my outcome was to provide the same game plan my father did to the business clients I worked with on a daily basis.

We have a strategy of going into everything. I love my kids. I love all the teenagers that I have worked with. When I worked with my kids, we had a strategy. The strategy was to focus on the things that were going to make a huge impact.

I remember this one kid I worked with back in Michigan City came from the hospital. He was hearing voices. One of the doctors planted the seed that he might have schizophrenia. I said, "You can have schizophrenia's features, but you don't have schizophrenia. You're only 16 years old."

The first strategy I had was to educate him and show him the facts so he could buy in to my story, and make the change now. I had him read books and articles about 16 years old children who can only have the features but not schizophrenia. I wish we had the Internet at that time, which would have made things easier.

Each step of the way I had to educate him, build a lot of trust, and influence him to think he can get better now. I had a strategy in my head of what I had to do first. I had to first convince this 16 year old teenager to have hope while still telling him that the doctor had every good intention in the world for him to get better. He just had a different strategy than I did.

I asked him if he ever played chess. He told me that he loved playing the game. I further asked him what was his game plan or the best possible outcome of playing chess. He told me to get the queen and win the game.

After I asked him about chess, my next strategy was to have him see social proof people who get help and are living a normal life despite of what their doctor told them. I showed him countless articles and stories of people. I asked him what they all had in common. He told me and his voice changed. I told him the next day that I will first change his voice, so he will be in better control.

In the meantime I told him to write down 50 reasons why he must change now. I told him once I come back to work in two days, I will help him out. I also stated that if he cannot think of 50 valid reasons, I will not help him out. The next time I came to work, he had over 75 reasons of why he wanted to change. Now I knew he really wanted to make a change in his life.

He told me that his voices are very mean and always tell him to kill himself or others. I asked him if the voices were a loud or a soft voice. I also enquired whether the voice came from his head, heart or throat. He told me that it came from his head. At this point I wanted to gather some information up; again I had my outcome and strategy laid out before I started speaking to him. After I gathered up all his information, I then asked him if he does not want to get rid of these voices and how this will impact his life in a negative way in the next five years. At this point my strategy was to have him hit mental rock bottom, so he can feel the pain and change now and this is when change takes place. Then I asked him to visualize how his life would be in the next five years if the voices stopped and he's back in control. I saw such a huge smile on this young man's face. He told me about all the great and positive things about how he can study in school, and how his life will be so much different.

I realized now we had enough leverage to make a change now and make it last. To make this happen I had to use a lot of what I call NLP (neuro linguistics psychology/ programming) because I wanted to make a change now. When I used these tools, I had my certification for only two years. I went to my mentor at the time, Joseph McClendon III and asked him what strategy I should use to make a change with this client in one session.

The child told me that he heard the voices in his head and they were very loud. I knew I had to change his voices so he can be empowered. I used several NLP strategies to make this happen. I asked him if he had ever heard a sexy voice. He told me yes. I further asked him who it was and if he loved her voice. He told me it was Pamela Anderson. I asked him what would happen if Pamela Anderson took the place of his loud voice and how that would feel. He again had a big smile on his face. I explained to him that he was the writer, producer, sound man of his own mind, and right then I was giving him the controls so now he could control the voices. I told him to imagine that he is Steven Spielberg of his own brain, and then I was ready to show him how to use it.

Now since we had the ground work in place, my job now became much easier. I did an NLP technique which I worked with his voices. I replaced his negative loud voice with Pamela Anderson's sexy voice. We then changed the volume and the pitch. We changed every aspect because now he knew he was the Steven Spielberg of his life.

I took him through a process and completely changed his inner voices. After that, the kid never thought that he had schizophrenia. He had new voices and now he took full control of his life. I really believed this would have never taken place if I didn't have a strategy. I really believe that we need to plant more positive seeds in people's lives and give them the faith. I planted this seed in this young man life, and I know 20 years later the seed I planted, changed his destiny.

We have to change our strategy. Looking at my dad, he had a strategy for everything. His strategy was impeccable with that garden. I took the method of the strategy from the garden and I asked myself, "How can I use the same strategy in my life? How can I strategize my business? Strategize my relationship? Strategize by my looking out because here goes I know my outcome." I know my end result. The question I have for you is this: What is your strategy inside your life? As I said again, every area of your life will change. First, you need to come up with a strategy.

POINTS TO PIN DOWN:

Knowledge is only potential power: The right activity moves you closer to your dreams and goals.

As you know, my father activated the right activity every year to create his proven strategy to grow his successful garden. What strategy are you using to create success in your life?

Here are few questions you should ask yourself before moving to the next chapter:

1. What is the strategy you are using in your life now for your weakest area?

2. What are the first steps you can take to create your goals and dreams?

3. Write down your strategy in your business, your relationship and your health.

"*Knowledge paves the road to riches—it depends on which road you take*" Think and Grow Rich.

Chapter 4: Time Management

I really believe that I picked up my time management system from my father, because to show me as a child how to juggle two full-time jobs, being a great father, raising ten children, hanging out with his friends, being a great husband, going to all of his children sports activities, have a full-time time garden, and sometimes even working at another job over the weekend; required great time management skills.

After I look back at that list, I am amazed how a person could have done so many things, and made it look easy. As a child, my father and I would watch TV shows like westerns and martial arts movies. We would spend countless hours talking and he still had other children to speak with, two full time jobs, a strong relationship with my mother for 67 years, and still never missed a beat!

People always ask me how I can write books, run several companies, work out seven days per week, spend time with my wife and family and always seem to be able to manage my time. I tell everyone that it is because I had a perfect model-*my father.*

As a child, for eight months out of the year, I would see my father get home from work at 12:00 am midnight, wake back up at 4:30 am, go work on his garden, leave for work at 6:30 am come home for lunch at 12:00 pm and also to check on his garden, hang out with my mother, go back to work and then again come back home at 12:00 am and do the same process over and over again. Some weekends he would work at another factory job because he always stated that you have to always make an honest hustle and make money come in for the family.

Now, imagine my father worked hard jobs in factory. Most people only worked one job. Since our father sent us to private schools and wanted the best for us, he worked 16 hours per day for 40 years. This is what I call amazing; a person who can manage his time.

I remember one day I asked my father why he had a garden. His answer was that it was to feed his family fresh vegetables and to help out people in the neighborhood who don't have any money. This way he could be a blessing to them. He would also freeze the food for the winter time

He told me that you have to plan your garden every year, knowing what to plant and when. My father told me that certain vegetables need to be planted at a different time of the season. Everything had to be planned. My father also told me that one must have persistence and never give up when times get tough. He said that sometimes you will feel like quitting. That is the time when having persistence plays a huge part in success in your life.

When I reflect back on my father's teaching, I now realize how I came up with my time management system. I added a lot of my father teachings and really didn't realize it until after his death.

Having a garden seemed to be a big deal for me as a child, because you had to plant certain things at certain times, which meant planning and managing time. Since we were living in the Midwest, we did not have a garden all year around. We only had it from March/April until October/November because of the collard greens which can be eaten pretty late as they can withstand the cold weather.

After modeling my father, I created a time management system and I added in this personal development system from what my father taught me, spiritual principles that my mother taught me, along with all the mentors I had in my long journey.

The name of time management system is **The ODA Secret Place**. Let me break down the concept of this amazing system.

The **O** stands for outcome:

What is your end result that you want to accomplish? If we take my father in his garden, his outcome was to have fresh vegetables so he could feed his family. When he would plant the seeds, he would see his outcome by telling me how beautiful the greens tasted.

The **D** stands for Daily Method of Operations/Desire to serve others:

So with a daily method of operation, what will you do every day to reach your outcome? My father would water the garden every morning and night. He would put lime to kill the bugs before they ate up the plants. At times he would add fertilizer to make the plants grow. This would happen each and every day.

When I used to do counseling, people would tell me that they needed to find a date. I asked them what their **DMO** is. What are you doing to find a date? Are you looking or are you asking your friends? What places are you looking at?

Desire to serve others: My father lived and stood by this principle his entire life. He served the entire neighborhood with fresh vegetables. I would see him lend a helping hand to everyone who needed his help. I would see him show unconditional love for everyone he met.

Then we created the three P's:

1. Plan,
2. Purpose, and
3. Being persistent.
4. Act as is (act like you already have your goals/dreams)

My father had a plan of action and he worked his plan on a daily basis. My father also had a reason of why he wanted his garden. I have found out that more the "whys" you have in your life, the more closer you will reach towards your goal. The last P, is being persistent and this is a MUST. If you are not persistent, you will lose every time. It will rain on your parade; you will be defeated sometimes before you even start. I really believe it's a must to develop the three P's if you want to accomplish anything in life.

So when I help people who are looking for a soul mate, I ask them as to what their plan of action is. If you are attempting to find a nice person, what places are you going to look? For example, is it the book store, church, having friends introduced, or in the mall? You must have a plan of action to find your soul mate.

Then I would ask my client as to what is their purpose or in laymen terms "why" do they want a soul mate? I had them come up with 50 reasons!

The letter **A** in the word ODA stands for Act as is:

At this stage, this is when you get your miracles. You talk about your goal, you tell your friends, you have now a knowing, and an expectation that you will accomplish your goal.

This is what my father did. He acted *as is* in his garden and every area of his life. He would talk to the plants and make them grow. He would tell me that in two weeks we will be eating from the garden, and we just put down the seeds.

We would sit down, and he would tell me, "Son, look at my beautiful garden."

The only thing I saw was dirt. Several weeks later, the thing which I termed as dirt, transformed into a beautiful garden.

When I speak to people who want to find a soul mate, I tell them to act *as is*; having a knowing that you have already found your soul mate. I am not giving a hope, because you move your body in a different way. I am not saying you wish you might find a soul mate. I am saying "act as is" you expect it.

When Jesus performed miracles and thanked His Father in advance, he had a knowing/ expectation that he will heal someone. Can you imagine Jesus saying "I hope I can heal you, I wish my father can heal you."

Not at all! So we need to model Jesus or your higher power, and act *as is*.

Using this time management system with my business coaching, I have increased my clients business by 100% to 2000% in a short period of time. I teach them how to tap into their higher power and break the chains of slavery and become free again. One of the teens I coached used this system and he graduated with a double major in four years with a 3.1 average. I challenge you to use this system and I guarantee that your life will never be the same.

POINTS TO PIN DOWN:

My father juggled two full time jobs, worked on his garden full time; spend quality time with my mother, his ten children, as well as his friends. As you know this takes time management skills. Here are few questions to activate your own time management system in your life. Please answer these questions before going to the next chapter.

1. What time management system are you using right now?

2. Do you have a to-do list?

3. What is your plan of action?

4. What's the purpose of your goals (why's)

5. How can you create more persistence in your life? Write down ten ways.

6. What is your DMO? (Daily Method of Operation)

7. How many people did you serve today?

8. What is your outcome in every area of your life?

Chapter 5: Passion

Passion implies a powerful or compelling emotion or feeling as love or hate, strong amorous feeling or desire, love, and or strong sexual desire, lust, an instance or experience of strong love or sexual desire. It also means a strong or extravagant fondness, enthusiasm or desire for anything.

My father displayed his passion 24/7. He worked all of the hardest jobs for 16 hours per day, and he would wake up 4-5 hours later to work on his garden. I remember when his garden was over and we started getting snow, my father would still wake me up at 4:30-5:00am just to talk about his garden. I knew so much about a garden that I could have worked on a farm. The passion and the desire he had about his garden and of course his family was amazing.

What I did learn from my father about passion was that he loved his job and his garden so much. I had never seen him complain about having to wake up in the morning to go to work, or any complaint at all. My father's work became his play. My father put in so much enthusiasm about living that it seemed contagious.

In my own life I am passionate about what I do. I have a burning desire to help people succeed, in any calling, because I guess this is how I am wired. I sometimes work 16 hours per day, and wake back up to work out 4-5 hours later.

I remember when I first went to an Anthony Robbins seminar about 20 years ago; I knew what I wanted to do with my life. I wanted to give seminars and workshops worldwide. Now think back, I am the same guy who had a stuttering problem, once I told my friends and they laughed at me. They told me I am a dreamer and I needed to stay at the mental health job that I was working at that time. Again I had the passion, I didn't know how I would accomplish my dreams and my goals, all I knew was that I would someday.

I would visualize myself on stage giving speeches to thousands of people. I guess I would use the same technique my father did with his garden. When my father would just put down the seeds, he would tell us about his beautiful garden.

So after I got back from my seminar, I told my then boss, Carl Scott about what took place. He could see the passion in my eyes and like a good boss, he gave me the green light. So what I did was I started changing the way I did my groups. I had my groups become more uplifting with lots of energy, something very different in the mental health field.

I thought I could try my new style with at risk with teens as they would tell me the truth and I could hone on my skills as a speaker. Most of the time in the mental health field people would do groups one to two times per week. I would do group four times per day for 12 years.

After a while, I was known for my groups and making a change in people lives at my job. I started getting more techniques like NLP skills, and going to more of Anthony Robbins' seminars. I had so much passion that what I did, never seemed like work. I had fun doing what I love: *helping out people.*

Then my world changed. I met and teamed up with Joseph McClendon III, Anthony Robbins head trainer. My skills in the personal development field went through the roof. I did groups all day for the entire weekend. The amazing thing was that the teens had a great time, and they got so many insights in there issues. My skills as a NLP practitioner grew as well. I could do one session therapy for any behavioral challenge. I spent my time reading countless books and attending several seminars. I had so much passion about learning, growing and changing people's lives that it became my obsession.

I started promotion of Joseph McClendon III, by doing seminars and workshops. I watched Joseph on stage and then created my own style. I used the same style I had with working with teens, because that worked for me, and I wanted to be authentic and true to myself.

Around the year 2000, I started doing seminars and workshops with business people. The dream I had back in 1994 became a reality. I overcame my stuttering problem. I changed the meaning and I realized that everyone stumbles across his or her words. I had a burning desire and passion to be like Anthony Robbins and Joseph McClendon III.

I still provided mental health services back in 2000. I started providing weekend workshops for pre-teen and teenagers. This process became a huge success. I would really turn decades into days. My teens would come in Friday, not really wanting to be there, and by Sunday they didn't want to leave. Think about it; if you can keep a teenager's attention for the entire weekend and they love it, you definitely have some serious skills. I continued to provide seminars and workshops to parents and teens. I started studying Jay Abraham's material in 1998. He was a marketing genius. I received some of his tapes and videos and I went to see him at Life Mastery during one of Anthony Robbins big events. I now wanted to be like Jay. I told myself that I already have the personal development and mental health. If I can add what Jay teaches for the business part, I would be unstoppable.

I read all of Jay's books and I understood his concepts about 50/50. 12 years later I received an email. At the time I was doing business coaching also. I thought my skills were amazing. A guy named Chet Holmes mentioned that he was looking for some business coaches and he worked with Jay Abraham for many years and on top of it all he said that I could make up to $250,000 working from home!

I read everything I could about this guy named Chet Holmes and I found out that Chet and Jay really taught the same stuff. Of course the words changed, but ultimately the matter was the same. Now you must realize that Jay Abraham is the master and he taught Chet Holmes years ago.

Before I did my interview with the Chet Holmes team, I did my homework well. I passed with flying colors. We started doing an intense training during the day. At night time I worked the midnight shift at a mental health hospital as a counsellor only making $12.00 per hour.

I studied Chet's information like my life depended on it. I had the passion to work midnights and get 2-4 hours of sleep and then work with Chet Holmes organization. They told me that it would take six months to make some serious money. I told myself that I would do it in three months. Just like my father taught me, I have to plant seeds and I must have an expectance of what will happen.

Three months later I quit my midnight job and was only working for Chet Holmes. I made seven times more money with Chet Holmes than my previous midnight job. I had only been with the company for six months that year and I ranked in the top 5 coaches.

The following year I started doing a lot to train other coaches, showing them what worked for me, and I would see coaches close $2500 to $10,000 per month. This did not take place that often before I came. I didn't act like your typical business coach. I had the personal development side of Anthony Robbins and now the business side. I had so much passion about what I was doing. Sometimes other traditional coaches didn't know how to approach or deal with me.

I stayed with the company for five years. I have trained several coaches and so many of them became the top business coach and consultant in their respective fields. All the companies who worked with me over one year have increased their business 100% to 3000%; this is what I am most proud of, working with Chet Holmes. After Chet Holmes died, the company had several CEOs; the company had big shoes to fill. One of the CEO's named Tom, gave me the biggest gift. He told me I act like Anthony Robbins with so much energy and that I don't act like a business coach. Eventually he fired me. I took that hit as a gift. Now my new passion is to take over the business coaching field. Since my business partner Chet Holmes died, someone must fill the space. I know if I planted the right seeds and do just like my father did in his garden; I will produce the same results.

I remember hearing a story of Chet Holmes. He always wanted to be business partners with Anthony Robbins. Chet looked up to Anthony Robbins. The first year he tried Anthony mention that he likes what he is doing but he just didn't have the time. It took Chet 17 years to have Anthony as a business partner. How many of you guys would spend 17 years chasing one person? This is what I call passion. He had a burning desire to do business with him. People would say he would visualize it, he talked about it and in his mind he became business partners with Anthony Robbins.

How many of you would spend 17 years pursuing one person? How many of you would have the passion of not losing faith and knowing this will work out for the best? How many of you would do what it takes to make things happen?

I remind you to stir up the gift, fan the flame. I'm going to stay passionate about what God gave me. Timothy 1:6

God gave us gifts. God gave us a lot of things to make our lives more passionate. A lot of times, people don't actually use their passion on a daily basis. A lot of people take their passion for granted.

Here's what my theory is: It is only a theory now, guys. I think all these people want to play basketball and God gave them the tools and to play basketball and the passion to start playing basketball.

I believe that God took all those talents and gifts and gave them to Michael Jordan because that's how he became so great. Michael Jordan, Larry Bird, Magic Johnson, Doctor J, Moses Malone, the list goes on. You've got to have passion.

You know when I'm a speaker, I have so much passion. I'm like in a completely different world. A lot of times when I'm speaking, I might have given a speech 10,000 times, but I give each speech with equal passion. I practice like it's my first time so I can keep the passion going on a daily basis.

What are you passionate in? How do you bring out your passion inside your life? What are you passionate in your business? What are you passionate in your relationship? What's your passion with your kids? Passion is the key.

My dad was so passionate about his garden. He would show people around the neighborhood his garden, his tomatoes, his greens. He was passionate about it. He had the enthusiasm. He had that excitement. What are you passionate about in your life?

POINTS TO PIN DOWN:

My father had so much passion about his garden, he would talk about it and he would show everyone who came by the house his garden. In the winter months he would create a game plan of what to plant next and or different. My father had so much passion about his garden that it became his hobby. Here are few questions. Before you go to the next chapter please answer these questions.

1. What are you passionate about in your life?

2. How do you activate your passion?

3. Make a list of everything you love to do.

4. Write down a list of things you will do and love without getting paid for it.

Chapter 6: Have an Attitude of Gratitude

Thessalonians 5:18King James Version (KJV)
"In everything give thanks: for this is the will of God in Christ Jesus concerning you."

My father had an attitude of gratitude about everything in his life. I remember as a child, during spring he planted the garden right around Easter time, and two weeks later we had snow. Please understand we are talking about the Midwest now, so my father's entire garden was wiped out.

The next day my father starts telling me what he's grateful for. I looked confused because I would have been angry, upset and cussing up a storm.

He told me, "Son, I am so grateful for we still have a garden. We have better weather, we now have sunshine."

My father focused on what he was grateful for instead of complaining. I also remember once we replanted the garden and he told me how beautiful his plants would be. I would have to say this was probably the best garden we had in many years.

All through my life this is what I have witnessed. I remember hearing my mother as a child praying to God for all of her extremities working. She would thank God for her waking up in morning, to have a sound mind, as well as for her kids to be safe.

When I worked in the mental health field, the population I worked with throughout my entire career were pre-teens and teenagers. We once had a young girl around 14 years old. She came from an abusive family. She had depression, some suicidal attempts, and school issues.

I remember one day in group I asked her what she was grateful for. She looked at me and said "With my life what can I be grateful for?" She then said that her father raped her, she tried to kill herself several times, her mother called her a slut, and she hated school. She mentioned that with this kind of life what one would be grateful for?

I told her that she could be grateful as she woke up this morning, did not get pregnant when her father raped her, she can be grateful as she is still in school, and the school authorities didn't kick her out, she can be grateful for getting help now, instead of being dead. After I gave her my list of things to be grateful, I had all the teens do an assignment. For the next seven days I asked them to write down everything they were grateful for in their life. I explained to them every time you show the negative emotions such as anger, worry, fear, stress, any negative emotions you must STOP and then say out loud ten things you are grateful for in your life.

To my amazement, during the next couple of days I witnessed a huge shift in these young adults behavior. A lot of their behavior changed. They seemed to have some pep in their step, smiled more and looked much brighter. It seemed like we had two set of young adults come to the hospital. When we came to day seven, these young adults had an entire different attitude. What made them upset in the past, didn't faze them anymore.

I had a 1 on 1 with the young adult who had all those challenges. She told me how those incidents had changed her entire life and that now she focused more on being grateful. When she does get in those negative emotions, she STOPS and focuses on what she is grateful for at that moment.

I explained to her that this was called "interrupting her pattern." Imagine a CD, if you take it and continue to scratch it several times with a nail and if you attempt to play it again it will not play the same. I told her the same thing happens to us. When you play the song called depression, if you take the nail and scratch it (in this case the nail is called "your list of being grateful"), then when you try to go back being depressed you can't. The girl named Sharon stayed at the hospital for 21 more days. Sharon's results were outstanding and she had been on the highest level. She was a role model in the hospital.

She started a grateful journey and wrote down what she was grateful for and how she helped and or impacted one of her peers life.

Since Sharon had been there for six weeks, we were at a time for discharge. I met her parents for a family session. When we started the family session, Sharon told everyone what she was grateful for. She mentioned five things about everyone in the session. We started talking about some serious issues that happened in the past. This time she smiled and told her parents she learned her lesson by the choices she made. Again her parents told me what had happened to Sharon and asked how she had changed so much. We started talking about the abuse from her father raping her. I believe this was the first time she confronted him. The mother at first took up for her husband and then with more detail her mother start believing what Sharon told her. The strangest thing I have ever seen is when Sharon mentioned what she is grateful for and her list surprised her parents, including me.

Sharon mentioned that this wouldn't have taken place. She would have never got help she really needed. She stated that she met some great staff members who really pushed her beyond her thinking. She was grateful for now having a relationship with her parents, she made this huge list, and then she told everyone in the session that she forgave her father for raping her.

Tears came from my eyes and I realized at that point it was time for her to leave. She was ready to get on with her life. Ten years later I found out that she was working as a social worker for the mental health hospital.

"Create the life you must have by having an attitude of gratitude. When life throws you a curve ball, find five things you can be grateful for and then start giving God a praise party. Then put a big smile on your face" ---Dr. John Oda

I remember late in my father's life when he was 87 years old, he became legally blind and had his leg cut off in the same week. This was the same time I moved back to Indiana to help out. I remember speaking with my father. His mind appeared to be sharper than a nail and seemed like from the outside that his body seemed to be falling apart.

What I took from my father is the positive attitude he had and how grateful he seemed to be from losing his eye sight and his leg in the same week. My father and I had a lot of conversations.

He said "I never thought that I would be like this in one million years, and son you need to pursue all your dreams and goals now."

Then my father told me what he was grateful for in his life; being married for 64 years at the time, having ten children and 86 grandchildren. He was grateful for working and providing for his family and sending us to private schools. He would tell me to always thank Jesus for all my blessings. He mentioned that he was grateful for the food he ate. He also told me he was grateful for his children helping him out in his time of need. He told me he was grateful for all the prayers offered by his family and friends.

At first this shocked me. Most people would have been so bitter and would hate God. My father was totally the opposite. When I would ask him how he was feeling he would tell me "I am doing 100." Sometimes in pain, he would still focus on what he's grateful for in his life.

I remember having my coaching sessions with my father when I moved back to Indiana, and I believed he planted many seeds in my garden at this time. My father would coach me about life, business, about my relationships, and he told me it's all a garden. He told me son, what seeds are you planting in your life? My father asked me what I was grateful for in *my* life.

He told me, "Son stop focusing on what's wrong, it's time to focus on what you are grateful for in your life."

Now the funny thing is that for about a week when we would have our talks he would ask me what I was grateful for and then he would give me my coaching session. This made me realize I must always focus on what I am grateful for in my life and when things get bad, I can always realize of what I am grateful for and have an attitude of gratitude about my life.

I remember the last couple of months of my father life; my sister Romaine told me he was not doing well. I remember I would send my father an audio and I would tell him how grateful I am for having him in my life. I told him if I can be 20% of the man he was, I would be a damn good man. I would send my father an audio clip bi-monthly; each audio clip would be for about ten minutes. I would give him a sense of encouragement. I would plant seeds in his garden giving him the will to fight this health challenge he was facing.

My sister told me after she played my audio he would have a smile on his face. Every word I told him came from the bottom of my heart. I wanted him to know how I felt. I wanted him to know the impact he had on my life, I wanted him to know that what I am today is because of him.

What seeds are you planting in your garden? Are you planting the seed of being grateful for what your higher power has given you?

My father told me to look at every area of my life and evaluate what seeds I was planting. In some areas I had to replant my garden so I could reap the rewards of my new and improved harvest.

I challenge you to find what you can be grateful for in your life. I challenge you to stop focusing on what's not right and focus on what you are grateful for in your life and what you have. Make a list of what you are grateful for in your life.

I found out in my life that once we focus on what we are grateful for, it changes the energy. In other words, it changes the vibration from focusing on something negative to focusing on something positive. What I do know is that it's all about the vibration you are in, so what I challenge the world to do is once you are in a negative state, stop and focus on what you can be grateful for in your life and I know your life will never be the same.

POINTS TO PIN DOWN:

My father had an attitude of gratitude even in his darkest hour he focused on what he's grateful for in his life. After watching my father, I realized that the best way to change your vibration is to focus on what you are grateful in life. Before you go to the next chapter, please answer these questions.

1. Make a list of 50 things you are grateful in your life

2. Make a list of five things you are grateful for in your family, business, career, health.

3. Whenever you are sad and or anger, stop and focus on three things you are grateful for in your life.

4. What dreams or goals have you stopped pursuing?

Chapter 7: The Desire to Serve Others in the Highest Way

My father served others in the highest way. If you think about it, biblically, what did Jesus do? He served others in the highest way. When I was a kid, as I told you, I had an idea to open a business with the garden and sell it. My father told me he was not going to sell his food; that he would just give it away. I told my father we could make more money selling the food and probably run some of the small stores out of business. My father refused and said that if you give it away God will bless you more.

I remember as a child my father would go to people's houses in the city and give them food from his garden if they didn't have a job or had lots of children or if they had a bad situation taking place.

I remember people would come by the house and say "Mr. Odessa, can you get me some greens?"

My father would tell me "Boy, pick some greens now."

I would think in the back of my head, we work in this garden and people don't help out, and now we are giving food away for free and we are not charging them for it. As a good son, I never told my father what I was thinking and I would just pick the greens and smile.

I remember as a child my parents would help people so much. My mother worked at St. Anthony's as a nurse and when people would get sick she would help them out, tell them what to eat, and then check on them. I would always wonder why my parents were doing these services for free.

When I grew up, my major focus was on chasing money. I wanted to have the Oda Towers everywhere. For over 40 years, I used to only chase money and then I realized it's not about money, it's about service. At that time money was my master and I was the slave. Now I am the master and money is the slave. When you focus on service everything changes. It's not about the money; it's all about the services you provide.

Think about it; when Jesus performed a miracle he said, "Thank you father," and then he had a knowing that He could perform the miracle. He didn't have a hope or a wish; he had an expectation. Then Jesus focused only on services. In my theory it's all about modelling. I have seen what my parents did and I read the Bible. All through the Bible it mentions about serving and changing your mindset, over and over. So my question is why haven't we adopted this concept in our lives?

When I work with my business clients and let's just say they want to make three million dollars per year but currently they are making $500,000. If they say I am going to make one million dollars, their brain will tell them NO. I tell my clients we must trick our brains and the way to do this is to only focus on services. I tell them if your average client is worth $5000 in sales, then you have to service only 600 clients. Now I tell them to put the focus on serving 600 clients and from there, we create a program based on serving 600.

In the chapter on Time Management and Mindset, we will help out on creating a game plan and incantations to support you getting your 600 people. It will look something like this.

"Thank you God, I, John Oda, see hear, feel and know I am so happy and grateful I am serving 60 people this month. I have sold (put in your services and or product) now, I am so happy and grateful I am serving 600 people this year. I have sold (put in your product and or services) by December 31, 2017." (Or sooner and or sometimes I would say NOW instead of putting the date)

When you say this with feeling and emotions, having an expectation to create this in your life just like my father's garden, you will reap your harvest. The most remarkable thing is when my clients would do this simple concept; their business would explode in such a short period of time. I really believe everyone must focus on service. When this takes place, shift your intentions and create powerful results in your life.

A lot of the time people get angry about professional athletes making so much money, and I took challenges by some people's statements. Now, let's take one of my favorite basketball players Michael Jordan. His last two years at the Chicago Bulls he made 30M per year; a nice income. Let's break down how many people he served: millions of people watch him on TV, people bought his jersey, people went to the basketball games (including myself), saw him on commercials, saw him on magazines, on boxes of cereal, and so much more. He served maybe 30M people or more per year. Let's say if he only served only 30M and if everyone paid him just one dollar, he made his money. One of the biggest reasons why is because he served more people. If you want to make what a professional athlete makes. It is all about serving more people.

If you want to make your business grow, if you want to make your life grow, it's all about service.

Give 10% to your church. Start off, if you're not making much, start off at one percent or two percent. When good, go up to 10%. I bet your whole life will change.

It's all about serving people in the highest way. My whole philosophy in business is the desire to serve others in the highest way. It's all about service. It's all about service and serving my God.

So how can you have a desire to serve other people? Let me explain it to you. The secret to making the most money in the world is to have all the happiness in the world by serving other people. It's giving people your time. It could be financial; it could be your wisdom.

It could be going to a nursing home and just talking to these old people who have been around for so long. That's when you get your true knowledge. It can be giving money to a foundation. I'm working with a new foundation also because I want to serve others in the highest way.

What can you do to serve other people? That's the key. I have used the principles that my father taught me in my 50 years on earth in every area of my life and the sad thing about is that I didn't know that until he died. I take that back. I knew it a little bit around the last five or six years.

The strategy that I use for my companies to grow their business, double, three, four, five, six times, is the strategies that he taught me. The strategies that I use for my teenagers, that's what I learned in that garden.

I'm telling you, between you and I and the words that are in this book; it taught me so much about who I am. It taught me so much about whom I am as a person and who my father was as a person, my biological dad.

Again, this book is dedicated to my dad. Write me letters, write me emails, and tell me how this book has changed your life, or maybe shift you in a different way or thinking, or made you understand how to tap inside your own seed of greatness. I want to thank you from the bottom of my heart. Take care and may God always bless you

POINTS TO PIN DOWN:

What I witnessed all my life was about my father serving others in the highest way. For my father, the more he gave the more it made him happy. Reading the book we understand that John Oda used to chase money and now he focusing on serving other people in the highest way. It's all about serving God.

As you know the NBA players serve so many people and their income is very high. How can you serve more people? These questions will activate a plan of how you can start serving others in the highest way.

1. Make a list of 10 ways you can serve other in the highest way (volunteer, go to a nurse home, help out your church etc.)

2. In your job/career/business, how many people can you serve per day?

3. How can you create a business of service?

4. How can you teach your family members as to how to serve others in the highest way?

Your Life is a Garden Action Plan

Eight weeks/days towards creating change in every area of your life.

1. Week one: What is your story? How can you replant your garden by changing your story? If you have a story of negative seeds of what someone told you, and or if you are in slavery like depression, worry, stress; when is now a good time to replant your garden?

2. Week two: Please do the chapter on faith; go over all your questions. Find creative ways to activate your faith, and have an expectation whatever you are seeking will come your way.

3. Week three: I really believe this is the foundation of all the chapters. In anything you must have the proper mindset. As you know it will rain on your parade and things will not go your

way most of the time. You will endure temporary defeat. At the same time once you say your incantations your world will be different. I really believe it is a MUST to say your incantations for 30-60 minutes per day. Remember to say them with feelings and emotions so that it gets into the subconscious mind.

4. Week four: What is your strategy in your life? Please do the questions and for the next week focus on a strategy. Find out what's going to work for you. Find out what's going to have the greatest impact to get you closer to your goal faster.

5. Week Five: It's a must to have a time management system to create success in your life. Please do the questions, and now looking at things and outcomes. I asked myself what my outcome was in everything I have done. This way I stay on point and hit my goals.

6. Week Six: Please do the questions on passion. Your work must be your play.

When you have passion you talk about it, you dream about it and you will do it for free. It's a MUST to find your passion.

7. Week Seven: You must have a desire to serve others in the highest way. It's all about service. Please go through the questions and find ways that can help you serve more people. Create a service journal.

8. Week Eight: Have an attitude of gratitude and please go over the questions. Create a list of everything you are grateful in your life. Every hour, read them when you are in a bad vibration like worry, stress or fear. Read your grateful list.

My hopeful outcome is to provide tools for people to make a change now; this can take you eight days, and or eight weeks. When you follow the book and apply the same tools in this book in your life, you will replant your garden. It's best to buy a journal so you can track and measure your success. Once you replant your garden, it's a must to add sunshine, create a positive environment, and add lime time to time and of course fertilizer. After you do this process and then condition this in your sub conscious mind, your life will never be the same.

Acknowledgments

There are many people I would like to thank for helping me along the way with my personal development and personal growth. I would love to thank my father Odessa Joseph Oda Sr; my mother Wardine Oda, my sister Romaine Oda who always encouraged me from day one to write this book.

I would like to thank my master mind group who helped me along the way and shaped my mindset, God, Seven Arch Angels, Joseph McClendon III, Anthony Robbins, Joel Osteen, Napoleon Hill, Michael Jordan, Bruce Lee, Oprah Winfrey, Andrew Carnegie, Jay Abraham, Chris Rock, Jack Canfield, and Chet Holmes

A special thanks to the following people for helping me along my quest.

Ajita John- Ajita helped me on my rough draft and helped me get my thoughts together.

Rebecca Bugger: Rebecca helped create my final draft, performing her magic to create this wonderful and powerful book we have right now

Carl Scott: Carl help me with my mindset months after my father died, and had me realize my gifts I had in my life.

Dwight Moxie: Became a true God blessing once my father died, open his arms, his family in my life. Became a true and honest friend at the most difficult time in my life. Someone I could lean on through the challenges I had to face after the death of my father.

Romaine Oda: My angel, who help me through the most difficult time in my life, who I could talk about my father on a daily basis. Romaine always seems to get me back on track with writing the book, and working my business. I want to thank the rock in my life, which listen with a caring ear, and planted positive seeds in my garden.

N3GU: I would like to thank my partners at N3GU Capital for having faith in me, and truly living our name and motto in our business and personal lives. " Never, Never, Never Give Up" I am very proud of all the successes we have created and grateful for our continued friendship.

I would like to thank all my patience and clients from the past and present for trusting me plant the right seed in your garden to make you grow in every way possible by walking my talk, and having you tap into your seed of greatness.

Dr. John Oda Companies

Profit Now Business Coaching

We provide business coaching and consultant for business we focus on several areas, creating systems, optimizing every business, sales, educational marketing, hiring, time management, Website/SEO, and creating profit centers. Our coaches will show you how to increase your revenue by 120% in 18 months. www.drjohnoda.com

Speaking Bureau

Goal setting, Communication skills, Time Management, Corporate Workshop, Human Diversity, Training, Sales Training, Violence in the Workplace, Leadership, Motivational/ Empowerment, Parents and Teens, and Youth programs. www.drjohnoda.com

Dr. John Oda is a partner with N3GU Holding Company. The following are our companies; www.N3gu.com:

InoLIfe Technologies

Is a publicity traded company a medical device company which provides needle free injector? We provide needle free injectors to doctors, medical clinics/hospitals, and consumer with the areas of dental, diabetes, local anesthesia, erectile dysfunction, vaccines/growth hormone, aesthetics/ beauty and Veterinary and Pets. www.inolife.net

Sanzo

Sanzo is a company from Canada we have the rights for Sanzo USA, this amazing product is a waterless car wash, bug remover, tar remover and dust cleaner, nanotech sealant for paints, tire shine and protector, cleaner and conditioner for leather and upholsteries, and degreaser. www.sanszo.com

All in now

Is an advertising agency that specializes in Facebook, LinkedIn and Instagram advertising? Using a proprietary algorithm and years of target custom list building. All in Now can select the most effective demographics for products services or people that yield the highest conversion in the industry, no matter what the budget is and we guarantee it or your money back. www.allinnow.ca

1-Material PTC

1-Material PTC is a company from Canada we have the rights for the USA. Is a company created under the parent company 1-Material Inc. that prides itself on innovative research and development. 1-Material PTC Inc. is dedicated to develop, manufacture and commercialize its Positive Temperature Coefficient (PTC) technology based materials and devices.

Our company has state of the art Research and Development facilities. Our team is built up of experienced scientific researchers with PhD qualifications specializing in fields of chemistry, material sciences, ink formulation, industry coating and electronic engineering. Building upon many years of Research and Development, 1-Material PTC Inc. has now commercialized its Positive Temperature Coefficient (PTC) based self-regulated heating products with the primary goal of making our living safer, healthier and more comfortable. www.1-materialptc.com

CPSIA information can be obtained
at www.ICGtesting.com
Printed in the USA
LVOW03*0029160916
504771LV00013BA/123/P

9 781634 914390